ECSTATIC HEALING

"As with Margaret De Wys's first book, *Black Smoke,* I was again unable to stop reading her second book, *Ecstatic Healing.* Not only is Margaret's story compelling in content, but she also takes her readers on a journey, sharing her hopes, fears, dark valleys, and ecstatic heights. The book made me alternately tremble and celebrate. Margaret allows herself to long for the transcendent, and in her courage and honesty as a writer, she helps the reader open up to their own spiritual longings and thus to the possibility of their fulfillment."

JOSIE RAVENWING, AUTHOR OF *THE BOOK OF MIRACLES: THE HEALING WORK OF JOAO DE DEUS*

"Margaret De Wys's *Ecstatic Healing* is a holy voyage—a remarkable testament of one courageous woman forced by her own sickness to discover the mysterious world of shamanic and spiritual healing. Hers is a journey of surrendering, a journey to faith, and a journey toward accepting herself as a healer. As in her first book, *Black Smoke,* Margaret writes with utter honesty, which helps us as we join her on her personal journey and question our own life journey as human beings and as healers."

ITZHAK BEERY, SHAMANIC TEACHER AND HEALER, AND PUBLISHER OF SHAMANPORTAL.ORG

ECSTATIC HEALING

A Journey
into the Shamanic World
of Spirit Possession
and Miraculous Medicine

Margaret De Wys

Inner Traditions
Rochester, Vermont • Toronto, Canada

Inner Traditions
One Park Street
Rochester, Vermont 05767
www.InnerTraditions.com

Text stock is SFI certified

Library of Congress Cataloging-in-Publication Data

De Wys, Margaret.
  Ecstatic healing : a journey into the Shamanic world of spirit possession and
miraculous medicine / Margaret De Wys.
      pages cm
  Summary: "Understanding ecstatic spirit possession for physical and spiritual
healing"—Provided by publisher.
  ISBN 978-1-59477-456-0 (pbk.) — ISBN 978-1-62055-171-4 (e-book)
  1. Spiritual healing and spiritualism. 2. Shamanism. 3. Spirit possession. 4.
Miracles. 5. Ecstasy. I. Title.
  BF1275.F3D4 2013
  203'.1—dc23
                                                            2012043243

Printed and bound in the United States by Lake Book Manufacturing, Inc.
The text stock is SFI certified. The Sustainable Forestry Initiative® program
promotes sustainable forest management.

10 9 8 7 6 5 4 3 2 1

Text design and layout by Brian Boynton
This book was typeset in Garamond Premier Pro

To send correspondence to the author of this book, mail a first-class letter to the
author c/o Inner Traditions • Bear & Company, One Park Street, Rochester, VT
05767, and we will forward the communication, or contact the author directly at
www.ecstatichealing.com, **www.blacksmokethebook.com**, or
www.margaretdewys.com.

AUTHOR'S NOTE

Although the story I am telling is true, names and places have been changed to protect people in Brazil, the United States, and South Africa. For the sake of the story line, I have condensed several months time period. My early travels to Brazil were made during the period of 2001–2003. During this time I also made several trips to Ecuador and Canada. In 2003 and 2004 I traveled to South Africa, Botswana, and Zimbabwe.

The soul should always stand ajar, ready to welcome the ecstatic experience.

EMILY DICKINSON

CONTENTS

Mediumship

Faith and Doubt

Be What You Are Called to Be

Mediumship

—∿—

*One doesn't discover new lands without consenting to
lose sight of the shore for a very long time.*

ANDRE GIDE

THE NECKLACE

September 1993, Rhinebeck, New York

It began with a string of beads, large, rounded, wooden beads painted white. The string was perhaps two feet in length—a simple, unadorned necklace without a clasp.

My friend Susan had invited me to a gathering at her house. Her home's architectural originality, like the majority of the houses in her shady hamlet, was created in the late nineteenth century. I walked into the octagonal backroom, a recent addition about forty feet in diameter. Red, blue, and yellow concentric circles were painted on the floor. This diagram was used for *vajra* dance, a Tibetan practice performed to harmonize the individual by integrating the body, the voice, and the mind in contemplation. *Vajra* means both "thunderbolt" and "diamond." My friends were Tibetan Buddhists and traveled in circles of spiritually like-minded people. There were fifteen other people there, most of whom I knew well. None of us really knew why we were there or what was going to happen.

Everything twinkled—the glass windows, the polished wood floors, the Tibetan bronze statues placed in a circle around the room. Candlelight illuminated the space. I removed my shoes and walked over to the only person I didn't know, a tall, middle-aged man who introduced himself as Brad. He was massive, bear-like but not at all fat. His hair was long and unruly, and he wore a kind of Hawaiian shirt and sweater combo over khakis. His smile lit up the room—I was immediately struck by his charisma.

Brad asked us to arrange ourselves in a circle. On one side of the circle was a makeshift altar. He turned to it and began moving rattles, stones, and feathers.

"Please don't touch any of these private artifacts," he said. Woo-woo time, I thought.

I'm not much of a group participant. I don't do workshops. Rituals and mystical experimentation en masse always put me in a rebellious mood. I saw in my companions a longing to believe in something transcendent. For my Buddhist friends the universe was populated with bodhisattvas, celestial deities who assisted and inspired them. What grace, what luck for them, I thought. I didn't believe I'd ever be able to follow any form of religion.

Brad began moving among us singing softly, praying, and laying his hands on some. He'd touch one person gently on the crown of the head, another at the shoulders, or pass his hand down along an arm. "I received a blessing and want to share what I've learned," he said. He began singing primal syllables—*oooos* and *eeees* and *ahhhs*. His voice was loud and penetrating, sounding almost like Native American chanting. It created a force in the room. The atmosphere sizzled. From the altar Brad carefully lifted a white bead necklace.

He approached one of the group members and invited him to touch the necklace, then—still singing—he moved to the next person, and around the circle, one by one. About ten people handled it. I smelled a kind of woodsy fragrance coming from Brad as he sidled over to me with the necklace. I reached out and touched it.

Suddenly my head jerked. My hands started shaking, then my arms, my torso, my legs. I lurched erratically as if electrocuted. I tried to break free, but the necklace held me. I felt as if a lightning bolt was inside me, and I was fused to it. I couldn't break away. Grunts and low growls erupted from deep in my gut and turned into howls. I spun around, still locked on to the necklace Brad and I held. I felt

I was being consumed by a powerful, mysterious force. I felt no pain. My mind was blank.

What was happening inside me was as uncontrollable as the contractions of childbirth. Some part of me—separate, watching—felt froth gathering at the sides of my mouth and bubbling over onto my chin. I focused on Brad's eyes, my mouth open in a bloodcurdling scream. His face grew large, intense. "Hold on to the power. Take it in," he said. Spit, honks, and rapid-fire utterances flew from my mouth. I shook even more violently. I felt my head snap back, seizing, and my body contorted into an arc. My body felt as if it was plunging from the top of a roller coaster, up and down again. Brad was holding the necklace; it still had me. Interlocked, we began whirling faster and faster, spinning in ever tightening circles. The room, my friends, forms, and colors were bleeding into streamers.

Suddenly everything stopped. I'd been unplugged. Brad and I were separated. My arms and my legs returned to me. I was stunned but once more in possession of my body. The charge in the atmosphere dissipated, and the group began to move about.

I was in a state of shock, but I felt very much alive. I looked at my arms and legs almost expecting them to have been charred by fire. What was that energy that ran through me? Why couldn't I let go? How could I be taken over with such force? I felt embarrassed, as if I'd publicly revealed a strange and intimate history long known between the force and me. It felt almost pornographic, worse than if I'd lifted my dress and peed on the floor while everyone stood watching. Mortified, I wiped the drool from my chin. Clutching the back wall, I slid outside the room.

Susan crept up, wanting to know what had happened. "Are you all right? You were shaking for at least five minutes." I couldn't find words. I felt exposed, humiliated, crazy.

"You're in control now," she said. My head was reeling. My body had behaved in a way I never would have imagined it could.

"Are you okay?" Susan asked again. She kept asking me questions, and I kept not answering; I couldn't. Finally, in my most composed voice, I said, "I don't know what happened. No language to describe it." I excused myself and went to the bathroom to hide. Inwardly I was vibrating at a high pitch. Half an hour later I searched for Brad.

"You must tell me about the necklace," I said.

"It's made of holy wood and once belonged to Credo Mutwa, the highest of the Zulu healers," Brad explained. "The great man placed it around my neck in a ceremony that marked my initiation as a *sangoma*."

"A sangoma?"

"An African healer, diviner, and clairvoyant."

"What made me behave as if I were exploding from the inside out?" I asked.

Brad told me of a rattle he'd once touched that caused the shaking inside him. "Just like what you felt," he said. "But after some minutes attached to the rattle I fell to the ground unconscious."

"I don't understand. What was that?" I asked.

"It's shaking medicine. Healing medicine."

"That doesn't explain it. I really need to know, Brad."

"One day you may learn. There's nothing more I can tell you," he said.

"Why not?" I asked.

"It's all heading somewhere, but you can only learn so much at a time."

Though I tried, I couldn't get more information out of him.

As I drove home I barely saw where I was heading. My God! What had happened? The power scared the daylights out of me. Confused as I was, I couldn't doubt what had happened. There were witnesses. That was good. And bad! They saw me like that. Something happened to me that hadn't happened to anyone else who held the beads.

I recalled at one point my eyes had rolled back into my head, my neck twisted to the right, and I'd foamed at the mouth. If I'd seen this happen to one of my friends I would have taken her to the hospital.

Brad hadn't seemed the least bit concerned. I kept reliving the moment, trying to figure out why, why, why. I felt as if something was pulling me into its world. Beneath my fear was a feeling of exhilaration. That force seemed to have picked me. The necklace recognized me. What did it recognize?

I felt like Regan in *The Exorcist*. A victim of demonic possession, she'd spoken in a basso voice, contorted into pretzel-like shapes, and her head swiveled 360 degrees. She had no control of her body; something or someone else was inside her. I don't remember if she was supposed to be conscious during the possession. I'd been conscious. But I'd felt no evil inside. That's the difference, I thought. Whatever power had seized me was not demonic. It seemed, instead, like a pure and powerful life force.

I pulled up to my house—a five-minute drive from Susan's. I had no memory of getting into the Volvo, or of traffic. I sat quietly in the driveway, engine off, not wanting to get out of the car and go inside.

My husband, Miles, and I taught at Bard College, a private college in Upstate New York. We lived in faculty housing, an 1829 two-story house. We'd been living together there since 1985. Our daughter, Lana, was eight years old. I'm a composer. He's a filmmaker. Life felt normal. Settled. We had the usual ups and downs of marriage but nothing extreme. He did his thing. I did mine. We had a good faculty life with dinner parties and departmental seminars.

I smelled skunk. It worked like smelling salts, pulling me out of my fugue. Our house, painted white with gray shutters, looked like a picture postcard. The porch light flattened everything except the potted red geraniums on either side of the front door. Crickets chirped and water gurgled in the nearby stream. I gazed at the four-foot-high milkweeds bordering the path that led uphill to the school library. There was a crescent sliver of moon in the sky. It occurred to me that I had to go into the house.

Lana looked up from her schoolbook as I came in the door. "I'm hungry," she said.

"Didn't you eat the dinner I made?" I asked, pecking her on the cheek.

"I don't want more spaghetti. I want something else," she said.

Miles was spread out on the black recliner watching TV. He nodded in my direction, then rose to get a beer. *He's up. Look at that play, folks. He's on the ten-yard line. Will he make the touchdown? Yes. He did it. The crowd is going wild! Man, oh, man what a play!* I was back in reality with a capital *R*.

"Miles, will you please turn down the volume?" I asked.

I went into the kitchen to make popcorn.

Okay. Everything is exactly as it should be, and I don't feel like I've been . . . I couldn't sort out what I felt, but I told myself everything was back to normal.

I made popcorn.

"How was your visit to Susan's?" Miles asked. He was watching a TV commercial—sexy nymphs and Coca-Cola—not really expecting a response. I had a dull headache. But the mundane scene helped me pull myself together. It also irritated me. I felt as if I were still gasping for air as I collapsed onto the couch. I wanted to tell my husband what had happened, but I was afraid he'd make fun of me. The irony was I could hardly blame him. I squeezed back tears. No way am I going to talk about the event at Susan's, at least not now, with a football game in the background. My body felt drained. Half an hour later Lana and I climbed the stairs and went to bed.

I couldn't sleep; the memory of the wild, unsettling sensations haunted me. I tossed and turned, fretting. I wished I had something to rub between my fingers to soothe me and imagined moving my index finger back and forth over the beads, feeling the smoothness. It was just a necklace, an African necklace. I wished this hadn't happened, but I wanted it to happen again. The raw power awakened my curiosity. Some reckless side of me recognized an urge to break free, to give in to compulsive desires and wild imaginings. Some part of me wanted to act. But how? Hours later I finally drifted off to sleep.

Near dawn I was suddenly awake and hyper alert. My nightgown was sweaty. A white light expanded and contracted in the middle of the room. I somehow knew that I should go outside. Miles was sound asleep, gently snoring. I rose and fixed the bed covers, the cool cotton sliding through my fingers felt reassuring, normal. Then I gathered my robe and slipped it on.

I inched my way downstairs. Light spilled into the dining room. It was only a mousy gray light bleeding through the paned glass windows, but my hands looked white and glowing, like porcelain under a florescent light. I opened the backdoor and stepped outside. The air was heavy, hot, and humid. Suddenly thunder rumbled.

The sky turned a bright orange, and birds, low-flying black crows, screamed overhead. *Caw! Caw!* Geese flew in formation, honking—as if escaping imminent danger. The trees and grass glowed, the colors and sounds unnerving me. I walked across the lawn in bare feet, feeling the dampness as I made my way to the hostas and wild rosebushes at the right of the yard. The birdbath was filled with algae and water. I felt enclosed and protected in the garden. I stood watching the sky, feeling a thumping and pounding under my skin. Lightning bolted above, turning the clouds neon green. The wind picked up and changed direction. I could smell the ions charging the air. A tunnel of wind caused an eerie whistling and low-frequency roar. I suddenly became aware that I could be struck by lightning. But once again I was frozen in place—it was like the experience with the beads was happening all over again.

I shivered with fear. Lightning flashed again. Closer this time. I somehow knew it was coming from Susan's house, where Brad was staying. It was coming from the beads. Again I felt something was after me. Images flickered through my mind. Then, standing in the yard, my nightgown plastered to my skin, blown by gale force winds, I remembered the dream I'd had before the white light woke me.

Crocodile teeth floated in black space. I knew the teeth were African. I said to them, how funny you are showing up in my dream. A black man appeared in a tangle of dense brush and gnarled vines; it was impossibly green, lush, and tropical. Underfoot the dirt was red. Wearing a leopard skin draped over his shoulder and with an air of great authority, he looked straight into my eyes. Credo, the witchdoctor—high Zulu priest—I knew it was him, calling to me.

Before last night I'd never heard of Credo Mutwa.

In a moment of utter sobriety I walked into the kitchen and put on a pot of coffee. My mind was clear. I began pacing from the kitchen to the dining room and back. It seemed unwise to take anything I'd seen in the last hours too literally or to jump to any conclusions, equally unwise to discount the events. I stopped pacing and looked out the dining room window. The sun was out now. The sky was clear. A male cardinal landed on a branch near the pump not far from where I stood only half an hour earlier. It tilted its head in a way that made me think it saw better out of one eye than the other. Was I projecting that onto him because I'm blind in one eye?

I have one brown eye and my left eye, the blind one, is blue. I contracted a virus as a teenager, and over the years my sight in that eye had grown progressively weaker. Despite two cornea transplants, glaucoma surgery, and cataract surgery, I became completely blind in my left eye.

I decided I should write out what had happened the night before. I got out a yellow legal-size notepad intending to make three lists—what had happened at Susan's, the dream, and anything from my past that might shed light on the evening's events. First, what happened at Susan's:

1. Shaking caused by an object, a necklace of African beads.
2. Loss of control.
3. But, I was aware.
4. No thoughts while I was being electrocuted. Frontal lobe activity? I don't think so.
5. Burst of vocal sounds. Like what? Sex moans? Cats in heat? Someone having the daylights beaten out of her?
6. Didn't happen to the others.
7. Brad is unconcerned, says it's happened to him.

Not very helpful, I thought. I decided to attempt the next list, the dream:

1. The dream is accompanied by weird weather.
2. I recognize Credo, the Zulu sangoma, in the dream and he recognizes me. What is the meaning of this dream, this person, and his relationship to me?
3. What does his name mean?

I pulled out my big *Webster's Third* and looked up the word *credo*.

It was a word of belief, of faith. His name was like a command to be acted on. Believe. Have faith. Maybe something was forcing me to confront my issues around religious belief. Credo, my credo, my faith had been in question for a long time.

I never made it to the third column because a realization slowly formed—the shaking and convulsing hadn't started with the beads. It hadn't started that moment in Susan's octagon. It had started a long, long time ago.

One summer afternoon when I was seven, picnicking with my family in an open meadow near Shelbina, Missouri, I wandered off toward a white tent I saw on the far side of the field. The tent was quaking, and weird, excited voices escaped. I approached, lifted a flap, and looked inside. There were a dozen grownups, people from "the sticks" as my parents would say. Poor but proud. A tall, boney man with dark, slicked-back hair, a plaid shirt, and dungarees raised his Bible. He wore a cap like a locomotive conductor's. The others looked like farmers: the men wore work boots, overalls, or jeans; the women wore cotton dresses printed with tiny flowers, dresses like my great-grandmother's. Hand-me-downs that had been washed threadbare. One woman's bottom teeth were missing, and her shoulders were hunched. Her silver hair was knotted in a bun on the top of her head.

The man with the Bible shouted and stamped his foot. People were clapping their hands, praising Jesus. Others were praying and begging the Lord to stop the suffering. People yelled and screamed. *The Bible says ye shall suffer. The Holy Ghost is coming down upon us in tongues of fire. We're gonna bind the devil. We shall cast out devils. Amen. Praise the Lord. Amen. Thank Jesus.* Amid the hand clapping and pounding feet, a man removed a brown-haired woman's glasses. She was shaking, stuttering, and hopping on one foot.

The Holy Ghost is upon us. Born again. We thank Jesus that we're born again. Spirit tell us what to do. We implore you. Tell us what to do. Praise the Lord. Amen. Thank you Je-sus. The hollerings intermingled in a febrile wailing. Shouts tapered and expanded in volume and pitch.

I lay on my belly squirming, glad none of them noticed me. I didn't want them marching in my direction. What I saw seemed too powerful, too alarming. The heat inside the white tent made me feel dizzy.

The frenzy increased. The brown-haired woman was rolling in the dirt, looking like she was hurt. People shouted, some getting hoarse. The silver-haired old lady swooned and collapsed on the ground. Gabbling commenced, like turkey squawks, and men and women began to shudder. More of them shook and rolled on the ground. Arms flailed in the air. People were bumping into one another, wailing, crying out. Dust was flying, and the strangest babbling I'd ever heard came from them. Their voices rose and fell like siren screams, revving and revving, fast and loud. The shrieks split through the tent.

I wanted to go into the tent, but I was afraid. I wanted to do what they were doing. It seemed so lively, so free. I loved the sounds. I loved the rolling on the ground. I wanted to roll and roll and roll. This Lord was exciting, fun, I thought. The rhythms, fervor, awe, and the holiness came alive inside me. I was magnetized. I felt these were my people.

Suddenly I was yanked from the ground.

"You must never go near these devil worshippers," my grandmother scolded.

"Who are they? What are they doing?" I asked.

"Holy Rollers. They're doing evil things. Co-trafficking with spirits is a dangerous sin," she said.

Grandma yanked me to the car. "That's the devil speaking through those people. They think it's God, but it's not," she said. But my body had responded to the quaking rhythms. I longed to shake.

Mom and I went to Sunday school and Bible school every week. We attended a cinderblock Baptist church with whitewashed walls, a pulpit, and hard benches. The church held about one hundred people. It had no graven images, no golden idols. It was the opposite of a Catholic church with fragrant, smoky incense, marble altars, ornate stained-glass windows, tables of flickering candles, sculptures prized for their artistry, swelling organ sounds, celestial choirs, and illuminated paintings of virgins. Our church didn't have anything resembling art, majesty, or wonderment. Such adornments were considered arrogant, sinful signs of depravity. The way of the Lord was humble, even severe. Our church's only decoration was a picture of Jesus above the pulpit. We had flowers only at funerals.

In Bible school we studied the teachings of Jesus. I aspired to embody Jesus's lessons in love. But the Lord Almighty, fist-in-the-air, unforgiving preacher gave me the feeling I was shrinking. I didn't like his vengeful God, his judgment, the doctrine of original sin, the exhortations to obedience.

My family was fundamentalist Southern Baptists from Missouri. Although we lived in Detroit, my mother was from hardworking peasant farmers, salt-of-the-earth types who feared God, damnation, and did a lot of praying; my father's family, also Southern Baptists, were more of the hell-raising type. My father's father, Red Daddy, was an ornery drunk. He'd shoot rabbits in back of the house, then with rifle in hand, rage into town. My relatives had names like Lottie May, Minnie, Uncle Cap, Aunt Nelle, Lamar.

My family's religion had strict rules about good and evil. Jesus was good; shaking and possession were the work of the devil. No playing cards, no drinking, no dancing—all would land one in the fire and brimstone of hell.

What I'd experienced touching the beads must have been like what the Holy Rollers had experienced when the Spirit came down in tongues of fire. Maybe I was reverting back to my bitter roots. When I touched the beads, I'd been possessed by a force much greater than myself, which I now realized was the same sort of possession I had witnessed in that tent all those years ago. I felt there was no evil in either place.

THE DREAM

1993–2001

Although the Zulu necklace had a powerful effect on me, and I obsessed about it for several weeks, my everyday life took over again. I had a young daughter, a house to run, a husband, friends, music to compose. I thought that was what I wanted. I'd get out of bed every day to tackle the same things I'd left off the day before. There was a roundelay of breakfast making, school bus waiting, house cleaning, food shopping, cooking, teaching piano, and music composing. Home meant comforting smells, daily clutter, cats lying on my music scores, the sense of belonging, the sense of being the fulcrum between my husband and my sensitive, bright child. She gave me joy. Miles and I were cozy, like brother and sister, had the same interests and loved traveling. The fact is, we both liked our life a lot.

I stored the experience with Credo's necklace in a far corner of my mind—or at least I tried to. In a haphazard, desultory way I picked up a book about shamanism. Then I ran into a friend who gave healing treatments. Curious, I asked for a session. Surprised to feel a mild current running inside me, I asked her what it was. She said, "Energy. Life force." "What does the energy do?" "Energy can be passed on and intensified in another person to initiate healing," she said. Immediately I was struck with thoughts about the necklace.

Over the course of the next few years I looked into holistic and shamanic modalities. But my dabbling became more serious in 1994 when I discovered the Robert Monroe Institute while reading Monroe's books. I attended a six-day intensive at the institute, a program designed to "expand one's awareness, and communicate with and visit other energy systems and realities." The institute used sound frequencies—which I thought might be a useful composing tool—to help one achieve altered states. While at the institute I had what appeared to be visions, experienced consciousness as being on the threshold of different existential planes, and felt my body morphing, vibrating, pulsating. The changes of consciousness helped me develop deeper sources of imagination and creativity within, and I began to trust my expanded awareness.

Two years later I discovered anthropologist Felicitas Goodman, whose specialty was religious trance. I worked with her at the Omega Institute in Upstate New York. "Ecstasy is a neurophysiologic state, a physical change that opens the biological door to the perception of alternate reality," she said. With her I achieved vivid trance states while enacting ritual body postures. While in trance I met an African diviner—in spirit form—who answered questions about the future. To this day whenever I hear a certain sound I find myself in this place where he lives, which I believe is in Mali or Niger. In trance I also traveled to Central America, Greece, and Siberia and met others—in my expanded awareness or in a world parallel to ours—who initiated me during ceremonies. I could visit the alternate reality Felicitas spoke about, and I continued meeting spirits while in trance states at home.

A year later another experience in shamanic tradition began working in the United States with a woman from El Salvador whose practices allowed her to see into the future and heal some diseases. In her presence I would spontaneously begin speaking in tongues—she would lightly touch my feet, nothing more. Another's voice would come through me! I recorded each personality. It would be years before I understood that I'd been possessed. I didn't know the value of my training at the time, but I had learned to discern which were helping spirits and which were not.

—⁄⁄⁄—

These extraordinary encounters were always percolating within me, but mostly I was home with my family, writing string quartets and chamber orchestras. The sounds I'd experienced at the Robert Monroe Institute, however, did have a profound effect on my composing. I began using specific frequencies in the music and listened to preprogrammed tones on headphones that altered my thinking processes while composing. I threw myself into my work. I had stopped performing—I'd played the piano—two years before to concentrate on my composing. I was creating sound installations in major galleries in New York. I had a commission to compose music for performances in Holland. I was richly productive and the work was fascinating, always leading to more curiosity and more work. I took every opportunity that piqued my interest.

But, at the same time, I was having unusual, occasionally extraordinary dreams. One night I had the dream that turned out to be the event that separated everything that came before from everything that followed. In this dream the vague figure of a man appeared. I saw that he was trying to tell me something. The communication was unusual, though I understood I needed medical help. "Cancer," he said, repeating the word several times. He pointed to my breast and showed me where I was sick.

I kept the dream to myself. It gnawed at me, chewed at the edges of my mind. It would not leave me alone, and finally, after some months, I went to see a doctor. I was diagnosed with breast cancer. The course of treatment offered to me was surgery, radiation, and hormone therapy. My husband was supportive, but I didn't want him to tell anyone. I spent days studying medical journals and researching treatments online. I talked to healers, scientists, homeopathic doctors, osteopaths, health fanatics, nutritional counselors, diet gurus, and wackos who practiced both in and outside the States. Treatments available included hyperthermia, IVs, mistletoe and laetrile therapies, ozone therapy, live cell analysis, juice fasts, and enzyme therapy.

I wrote music like a demon. To escape. To create. To feel alive. I thought, fretted, tried to find a way free of my fear. My diagnosis forced me to look at everything differently. It was like a big fireball—an explosion inside me that yelled, "Move!" I knew I didn't want to die, but I also realized that I wanted to feel alive again, really alive, in a way that I hadn't experienced since I was a child, since the beads.

Cancer. This was the showdown. The sharp shooters of the universe had me in their sight. Théun Mares wrote about the shooters in one of his books in the Toltec series. I didn't remember which book, but I clearly remembered them—mythic warrior beings. I knew what *sharpshooter* meant. We humans could get picked off or maimed at any moment. You could die. No guarantees. No wiggling out.

For the Toltec's the path of spiritual practice led through a harrowing gauntlet of human experience. According to Théun we had to rediscover our life's purpose and participate fully in life. In his first book, *Return of the Warriors,* he wrote, "We all have incredible abilities and awesome potentials which never surface unless a sword is dangling overhead."

I was running on the edges of my life. I had to come to terms with who I was, and I had to do it fast. I questioned all my various identities. None of those active in my day-to-day life could help me. I looked at my options. There was Western medicine, but I felt there were other healing modalities that I needed to consider. I tried to connect to the energy and feelings I'd come to understand in a small degree when I'd touched the Zulu necklace, when I was with Felicitas, at the Robert Monroe Institute, and with the Salvadoran woman. I didn't understand how these experiences would cure me. But my gut instinct was powerfully pushing away from allopathic medicine.

While I was figuring out what to do—surgery, radiation, hormones—I took a trip to a neighboring town. On Main Street, I ran into Janet, a woman I vaguely knew who gushed about a trip she would be taking to Guatemala to meet indigenous healers.

"That sounds phenomenal. How did you score that?" I asked.

"My Guatemalan friend in Boston invited me. There are going to be big ceremonies. According to Mayan prophecy all races have to be included in these special ceremonies. There won't be many of us whites there."

"How much does it cost?"

"$1,800. The price helps pay to fly healers in from South America. They'll be available for private consultations. The group is looking for one more person. Why don't you come?"

I felt like a thunderbolt had struck me. This was a gift from the gods. A miracle! I scribbled down the contact phone number. I decided immediately that I would go if they accepted me.

The colors, sounds, congestion, and delightful mayhem of La Aurora Airport in Guatemala City felt reassuringly alive. Native Americans had come from the northern Canadian Rockies down to the southern parts of Chile to participate in the Mayan ceremony for the New Year.

Carmine, a Mayan priestess, addressed the group—a dozen whites, a few Africans, a few Asians, and about twenty-five Native Americans—in Spanish and then English. "We are gathered here for the blessings of the Feathered Serpent and Waq'xaqi' B'atz', the New Year ceremony," she told us.

According to the Mayan calendar, we were entering the last Choltun, a thirteen-year transitional period before the Sixth Sun (each sun is a 5,200-year cycle), which would commence on December 21, 2012. The prophecies said the Sixth Sun would be a time of equanimity and equality between the races. The First Peoples would be restored, reinstated to their rightful role as guardians of nature. The sickness of the Earth, the sickness of tribes, and the sickness in each of our bodies were inexorably linked in the aboriginal mind, and the ceremonies in which I would participate were healing medicine.

"Leave your ego behind, for it will only interfere with your experience," Carmine admonished. After slapping us around a bit more she held out the prize. If we behaved respectfully, she promised us whites, "You will receive great wisdom." Not only that, "We have come together as strangers," she said. "But each of us will end up playing a historic role."

In Guatemala no one knew I was sick—but many healers were there. I kept quiet, waiting to decide whom I should ask for healing. And then a Shuar healer from the Amazon jungle approached me. He was bare chested with cinnamon skin, almond eyes, and a compact muscular body. He wore a brightly colored corona of red and gold toucan feathers and a bandolier of seeds that vibrated softly, like a rattlesnake, when he moved.

"I must speak with you," Carlos said. "I see inside your body—your veins, your organs, your blood, your cells. Black smoke is trapped in your breast. You must come to Ecuador, and I will heal you."

I was stunned. Here was my healer.

I went home, had a lumpectomy, and told my family that I was going to the jungles of South America for the rest of my treatment. "You're going *where*, to do *what*?" my friends and husband asked. "Isn't that a little bit *extreme*?"

Deep in the Amazon, Carlos guided me into a world of potent visionary plants, harrowing initiations, and ritual purification. This jungle world differed vastly from our own in its perception of healing and wholeness. Carlos treated the cancer with ayahuasca, an extract made of jungle plants known to induce visions. I went through a physical and emotional "holy voyage" as he called it. After a few months Carlos told me I was healed. I wept with violent intensity. I wept for joy. That experience was the beginning of my road toward being healed and healing, which I have written about in my memoir, *Black Smoke.**

I flew back to New York, thinking about raw jungle life and how much I'd benefited from the ceremonies and initiations. I marched off to the cancer center in New York. I knew I wasn't sick; I wasn't sure what the Western doctors would say about my condition. But I felt as if I'd defeated a monster and gotten my power back.

---

*For an in-depth reading of my Amazon experience see my book *Black Smoke: Healing and Ayahuasca Shamanism in the Amazon.*

"The cancer is gone. We didn't find a trace of it," the doctor said. I could tell he was surprised. "Holy shit," I thought. "There must really be something to this indigenous healing."

"But I'd like you to have radiation and hormone therapy. This is probably going to come back."

"I can't do that," I said. I refused radiation no less than three times. It occurred to me that he had to offer it and insist on every possible treatment. He didn't want to be sued.

Then he asked me what I'd been doing, and I told him I'd gone to the Amazon jungle for treatment. He bent in close, not wanting his staff to hear and whispered, "Whatever you're doing, keep on doing it."

His voice rose, "You'll have to have x-rays every six months." I thought back to Carlos's pronouncement that I was healed. I had my verifiable proof from the medical community.

Before Ecuador, I would have considered the jungle treks, fasting, initiations, and difficult purifications tests of endurance. I had seen spirits that had a transpersonal reality to them. I'd gone to another time and another place—to other realms that were just as real as what we see with our physical senses. I apprenticed with Carlos in Ecuador, where I was taught the stance of a warrior, how to cook certain medicines, how to reach powerful spirits, how to identify certain diseases, and how to look into a patient's body. I assisted him as he treated patients throughout Ecuador.

What happened to me in Ecuador was considered utterly improbable in my culture. Even I had once considered it improbable. But what I'd experienced defied both logic and science. What happened with the Zulu necklace and in Ecuador should not have happened if the universe were as science said it was. Realizing this turned my life upside down.

Carlos was living in Canada so I came back to the States. I tried to resume my life in Upstate New York, but I was a changed person. My daughter was away at an early college program. Miles and I spoke civilly to one another, but whatever we'd had together earlier in our marriage had died. We were living in different realities. Miles acted as if our estrangement was natural, ordinary, and acceptable. But I felt as if I'd transcended narrow boundaries to identify with a larger reality. There was a new me that even I wasn't accustomed to.

My marriage was over. The hurt was there. It wasn't going to resolve. The divorce unfolded graciously enough but was mired in sadness, isolation, and economic instability. I'd lost my home. But I'd been put on this circuit, and I didn't want to get off.

I'd been cured; life in South America was stimulating, exciting, more so than I'd experienced before Ecuador. I'd gone to a traditional healer when I'd gotten cancer. I'd learned a lot about aboriginal medicine. A door had opened; my imagination had been revived.

The urge to explore was overwhelming. It felt as if a guiding hand was steering me, had been steering me all along. I just had to acquiesce. I just had to say, "Yes."

At the same time, I struggled with what it all meant—going into unexplored territories, venturing into new modes of being. Something had shifted. I felt I was no longer on just a quest for physical healing— I was on a spiritual quest. I believed important information would be revealed to me if I kept searching. I accepted that there was a great unknown. I felt I had a personal connection to the ineffable even though I did not have a devotional spiritual practice. I believed in greater-than-self influences. Whatever message had come through me when I first held that Zulu necklace seven years before was slowly being revealed. And now I was determined to follow it.

Acknowledging these things meant actively pursuing my spiritual awareness and evolution, walking purposefully toward it. It wasn't like saying *I want to start my own company. I want to buy a house, or make an album or a music CD.* These were worthy obtainable goals, all material in nature. I had to understand where I was on my evolutionary path. This meant having faith that I would know when the time was right for action and know what action was required.

I was going to search out a deeper level: I wanted to allow spirit to inhabit me. When I'd touched the necklace it seemed as if I'd been possessed by a great force. I was drawn to the power. I was drawn to the beauty of it. I believed spirit, or what I thought of as a great presence, could heal a person, change her beliefs. Maybe it could even give me purpose. I just had to be ready, open, and in the right place. There seemed to be a hidden order, and I would be shown the pattern in due time.

It seemed the important things in my life always came without warning, without me searching them out. They appeared as accidents.

While thumbing through a *Shaman's Drum* magazine in the local bookstore, I came across intriguing photographs of a man performing psychic surgery. In the article Josie RavenWing described João de Deus, or John of God, as a mystery healer, or miracle man. Pictures showed João cutting into one woman's stomach, removing tumors from another person, and operating on a man's brain. Without anesthesia! Without sterilization!

What really got to me was a close-up of João with a knifepoint gouging into a man's eye, spread wide, vulnerable. He was performing eye surgery. I cringed in horror and awe. The article stated that John of God had to be possessed by a spirit to perform these surgeries. In his picture he looked unpretentious, like no one special. He wore glasses, looked to be in his mid-fifties, and was dressed in a short-sleeve shirt. He could be a schoolteacher, dentist, shop owner. João seemed like just another human being, I thought.

I learned he didn't charge for healing and that he'd worked on more than a million people. Testimonies from those healed of supposedly incurable diseases were his credentials. He was born João Teixeira da Faria in Cachoeira, Goiás, in 1942 to Portuguese parents, a tailor by trade and a devout Catholic from a poor, lower-class family. As a child he had clairvoyant abilities. He hadn't gone past the second grade, didn't read or write, and had never been to medical school. As a young man he'd traveled from village to village performing healings. In 1978 he settled his healing center, the Casa de Dom Inácio, in Abadiânia, where it still stands today.

If what I read was even remotely true, I had to see for myself. Thank God my cancer was cured. People went to John of God to restore their health. I didn't need my health restored. I was going to John of God for something deeper, something spiritual.

On Google I found Josie RavenWing and called her in Florida with every intention of going to Brazil for two weeks. I questioned her about the Catholicism at the casa. Josie reassured me that the casa didn't have rigorous, guilt-inducing religious ordeals.

I had enough savings to see me through for the next couple of years, and I decided I would use the money to take the brave path.

HOUSE OF MIRACLES

November 2001

The TAM Airbus banked over wetlands, palm swamps, and tropical mangroves. It felt as if the humid, lush green from below was seeping into my chest, bringing with it powerful memories of my last visit to the Amazon jungle. We'd soon be landing in Manaus, Brazil, situated three degrees south of the equator. I'd been two degrees south of the equator in the high upper Amazon in Ecuador, the other side of the continent. This was my eighth trip to South America but my first time in Brazil. The plane's wings tipped down. I could see the Rio Negro and the clay-colored Rio Solimões swirling, red and black silt colliding, as they flowed together into the Amazon River. A ribbon of tarmac appeared through the sea of lush green forest and brown, spidery waterways. Palm trees jutted against the runway, pushing through the concrete like weeds.

We landed at Edward Gomez Airport in Manaus, a white one-story building. On the ground the air felt like a blast furnace. Already the dull gray chill of New York, which I had left only fourteen hours earlier, seemed a lifetime away. I'd packed summer clothes, shiny lipstick, binoculars, a journal, my laptop, a tape recorder, and $3,000 in cash. There were no ATMs and no credit cards or travelers' checks accepted where I was going.

I flew on to Brasília, Brazil's capital, located in the central plateau known as the Cerrado region. Tropical plants and red birds of paradise were placed strategically inside the glass passageway that funneled passengers toward baggage claim. At the luggage carousel I met Josie, a slender, attractive blond with short, thick hair and dazzling blue eyes, which I thought might have been lined with blue tattoo ink. RavenWing was the name given to her by a Native American tribe, the Diné (Navajo) in Arizona with whom she had apprenticed. I'd read from her bio in the *Shaman's Drum* article that she'd been a dancer, a holistic psychotherapist, and an energy healer. She'd studied shamanic and other multicultural spiritual approaches.

There was a sense between us that we were of the same fabric. We'd exchanged normal society for pursuit of the numinous, the mysterious, the unknown. Josie was busy herding her tour group of sick people through customs. As she was directing them out of the airport she invited me to ride along to the casa. I accepted.

We boarded a bus for João's center, Casa de Dom Inácio de Loyola—named for Saint Ignatius—located across the high plateau of central Brazil. The trip along the BR60 four-lane motorway to Abadiânia—a place not found on any map—would take two hours. Soon after leaving the airport I noted the Olhos de Aguas Palace Hotel (Watery Eyes Palace Hotel) and the 1001 Noites Hotel (1001 Nights Hotel). Then we passed dowdy evangelical churches, tire stores, refrigeration businesses, Coca-Cola factories, auto garages, and *lanchonetes*.

The blue velveteen seat smelled of sweat. I inched toward the window as the bus wove and shimmied slightly. We were traveling at fifty miles per hour. People were chatting away, but I stayed to myself, my m.o. when I was in quiet contemplation. After what I'd read it felt as if I would be meeting the high Houdini of the spirit world. Only John of God, I'd read, was no trickster. He was a master of the spirit realm and healing.

After the industrial suburb we left the cityscape behind. The view broadened as green pastures and red earth expanded into the horizon. The Cerrado, or Brazilian Savannah, was punctuated by cactus, eucalyptus, and tropical trees. Rolling hills and ten-foot-high termite mounds, red granite-like pyramids, dotted the mostly empty but verdant landscape. The mounds continued on for miles and reminded me of pictures I'd seen of the African Savannah; pyramids up to thirty feet high of hardened stones teeming with millions of lives. Suddenly I thought of Credo standing on land similar to what I was seeing outside my window. But lions, gemsbok, and elephants surrounded him. The vision was startling. He seemed to want to get my attention—about what I wasn't sure. I was half awake, half asleep, jet-lagged, and I assumed the vision had been a daydream or reverie. But seeing him was like when he'd come into my dream wearing leopard skin. That seemed very real.

The bus driver made a right turn. I surfaced from my thoughts to see we were in town. Abadiânia is a dusty village of one-story buildings and a brick-making factory. We passed a small man in a Stetson hat driving a horse cart stacked with potatoes. The three wheels wobbled as the cart bounced. Rickety trucks and antiquated automobiles sidled through town. In front of a yellow concrete house the bare feet of kids scraped into the dirt—along with six or so chickens who pecked and scratched. A smattering of trees shaded the brilliant white sunshine beating down on the town. There was a mottled brown cow hobbling in a grassy spot, an expansive sky, and puffy cumulus clouds. Patients in wheelchairs rolled down the dusty streets. Dogs yawned. People and beasts moved slowly. There were no souvenir shops, no coffee shops, no pizza parlors, no adventure tours, and no tourist attractions. Our shiny modern bus seemed an anomaly, a ship from another era.

The driver pulled up to our *pousada,* Catarinense, one of many small hotels in town that served the people making this pilgrimage. It was pink cement, one of those low, squat buildings like a motel in the desert from the 1950s. Our hosts, Gentil and Valeria, of German descent, were accommodating and kind. But it took an hour to get the key that would open my small, sparse room.

"Put your bags away. Have a shower. Dinner will be at six," they said smiling.

My room was between the rooms of two women I met on the bus, one with chronic fatigue syndrome, the other a diabetic. I was jetlagged and not fussy like they were about the accommodations. I could hear Janet through the paper-thin walls. "Do they expect us to stay in this room without air conditioning? And this spongy bed, I bet I won't sleep a wink while I'm here."

Dappled afternoon light streamed through the shuttered windows. I opened them, letting in a blast of heat. The room had two narrow beds. After a cold shower—I'd brought a towel, soap, and shampoo from New York—I lay down and looked up at the ceiling where a column of ants marched toward the corner of the ceiling. There was a very ugly black worm crawling on the wall.

In the dining area I filled my plate with chicken, chayote, and potatoes from the buffet and carried it to one of the large tables. I sat with a dancer from California who had come because of high blood pressure, an acupuncturist from Germany, a man from New Jersey with a brain tumor, a woman from Colorado crippled with multiple sclerosis, and a nurse from Great Britain who had advanced breast cancer. I listened, in awe, to their stories, brave hopes, and fears. Tender comrades, I thought. Conversation at the table revolved around mysterious and mystical happenings at the casa—things people had heard of or witnessed or experienced themselves. I listened in quiet rumination, with a prayer in my heart.

The next day I walked down to see the casa. The wrought iron gates stood open. The compound, made up of several open-air buildings painted white and blue, was built from cement blocks. Disappointingly institutional but spotlessly clean. I hope I haven't come to a cult or religious center, I thought. I was seized with an edgy, resistant feeling. The casa environs, though peaceful and apparently comforting to some, smacked of church.

A few people milled about in the casa gardens. This was a day on which João was not in session. A giant bird of paradise plant with a red, furry top reminded me of the temple shapes at Angkor Wat. Mangos, jackfruit, pomegranates, and avocados dropped from dwarfed trees. Long-beaked hummingbirds drank from hibiscus bushes.

Sitting in the garden I was not aware of the poverty outside the healing environs. The casa created the local economy. People devoted to João who had been cured of terminal diseases moved to Abadiânia to be near him and started thriving hotel businesses. These people were inside the healing environs, which was cut off by the BR60 highway. On the other side of the highway was the impoverished part of Abadiânia.

I stood up and moved into the casa's assembly hall. It was a partially open-air pavilion with pillars, cement floors, wall fans, and a small stage where, I was told, people could watch João perform surgeries. An unused microphone stood off-center. On the back wall hung a wooden triangle about three feet high. Photographs and pieces of paper with loved ones' names and descriptions of the problems plaguing them were stuffed in the frame. A dark oval smudge in the center of the triangle had been made by people's sweat as they'd pressed their foreheads against the wall to pray.

A beautiful woman stepped away from the triangle. She passed me and without warning took hold of my hand. I looked into her eyes. There was so much tenderness, piety. Silently we walked back to the garden and took a seat in the shade. Her dark eyes were like liquid lead, her skin the color of caramel. She was forty-five, about my age, and Brazilian. As we sat in the dwindling afternoon light she offered me words about her most important relationship, with God. She spoke with tenderness about João and the spirits of light who worked through him. I learned her name was Ana. Originally from Belo Horizonte in the southeastern region of Brazil, she'd come to the casa for healing almost two decades ago. Now she was part of João's inner circle.

I trusted her and opened up. "It's very calm here. It feels safe," I said.

"Yes. It's peaceful and protected here." Her English was passable. There were the soft swishing sounds of Brazilian Portuguese in her voice.

She wanted to know why I'd come to the casa, where I'd come from. What drove me. All her curiosity was couched in simple questions, unassuming and innocent. I explained how I'd recently come from the jungles of Ecuador, about my healing, and the healer I'd apprenticed with there.

"I'm more comfortable in the wild, savage jungle. This place looks like a church," I said delicately.

"You'll get used to it. It's not at all like church."

"A hospital? I shun those places too."

"Well, this is a spiritual hospital, my dear." We stood up and began walking. "Come let me show you something," she said. We entered a small room next to the main hall. Stacked along the walls were discarded wheelchairs, walkers, and crutches.

"These were left from people healed at the casa?" I asked.

"Yes. Most of the good wheelchairs go to places where people in need can use them."

There were several photographs on the wall of João in the 1980s. In one he was with the famous Brazilian medium Chico Xavier. Chico had told João he should go to the small Goiás town of Abadiânia to fulfill his healing mission. He'd foreseen the casa and people streaming in for help. Another photo showed João seated. There was what looked like blood running down from his heart.

"What's going on this picture?"

"Several years ago John of God suffered a stroke and was paralyzed on one side. He was taken to the hospital and later relegated to a wheelchair. After three months of paralysis, during a healing session the entity inside him said to the audience, 'Now, we are going to heal João.' A scalpel was called for. João's hand took the knife and sliced into his own chest. He stuck his hand inside, near his heart, and pulled out a blood clot. When he finished, he called for a needle and thread to stitch the wound. Since that day he hasn't been paralyzed," she said.

"This photograph reminds me of Saint Sebastian. It's discomforting, potent. Surreal. Many saw João perform the surgery on himself?"

"Yes. I am told there was a large audience."

"He does physical operations, and then there're the spiritual ones I've heard about. Can you tell me more before I see him tomorrow?"

"With an invisible operation you'll be directed to sit in a room in the casa and meditate. João enters the room and pronounces 'In the name of God Almighty you are all cured. Let what needs to be done be done in the name of God.' The other type of operation requires that he cut into you. He doesn't necessarily cut where the sickness is. It's up to the spirits to decide."

I wondered if getting cut worked faster. Ana said, "No." I thanked her for sharing her knowledge with me, for telling me more about the healing processes. We hugged and split up, deciding to meet again.

I walked out of the casa compound, turning toward the open countryside. I followed the red dirt road downhill coming to a fork, which I took to the left. I continued walking down, down, down into the valley, wet with perspiration. Four macaws flew overhead, honking. They were streamlined, with slender tails like spears. Large yellow and black butterflies flew in circles. Their shadows flitted on the ground in crazy patterns.

I moved farther away from town, deeper into the countryside. It felt very solitary to walk in this wilderness with streams, gallery forests with purple trumpet-bushes, copal trees, pepper trees, prickly ash trees, and eucalyptus. Most spectacular of all was the view, a green bed of rolling valleys and hills that touched the clouds. I paused for a moment and looked out on the panorama of luminous green fields and rugged camel-humped hills. Cattle with bony necks chewed tough scrubby grass. The footpaths, like veins of rich red earth, were the color of blood. A pair of vultures circled in the thermals above me. The bush seemed to come alive, as did the mosquitoes.

After dinner I stood outside the pousada. The humped hills were domed in shadows. Josie and I sat on her porch enjoying a smoke. Mine was natural Brazilian tobacco wrapped in cornhusk. It was about seven inches long, and thin. We exchanged personal anecdotes. I felt close to her, and I could see she understood my work with Carlos in the Amazon. She'd spent nine years with the Diné. I asked for her help.

"What's it like going before John of God?"

"You may feel an energy buzz, Margaret. Some people get dizzy in the main hall as the spiritual work begins while they are waiting for their turn to go see John of God. When called you will line up with others and proceed into the first current room. As you walk through it you will be diagnosed by the spirit entities who work in that room and given a spiritual cleansing. John of God will be sitting, already incorporated by one of the entities, at the end of the second current room. You may feel an intensification of energy as you move toward him. The time in his presence usually lasts only seconds. Try to look him in the eye."

"I will do that. But why? Is this important?"

"His eyes change color depending on the entity inside him."

"You can see the change in his eyes?" I asked, incredulous.

"The color changes from blue to brown or green are striking. But the look is always pure, focused with concern for you. You might not notice his eyes; you might be in an altered state."

"Does he know what's going on when he's in trance?"

"No. His physical eyes aren't seeing anything. There's someone else seeing through them. It's very strange."

"How many entities are there?" I asked.

"There are thousands who work at the casa, but only thirty-some of them enter João's body and communicate through him. Each one of these entities are known by name. The ones I've most closely observed possess João are King Solomon, the first entity to ever incorporate in João when he was young—King Solomon's presence is so strong that

João's physical form can only sustain brief periods of incorporation," she said. "Then there is Francisco Xavier—he likes to do a lot of surgeries; there's Saint Ignatius of Loyola, head of Dom Inácio; and Dr. Augusto and Dr. Oswaldo Cruz, who were Brazilian doctors and surgeons in the past century. There are others who have their own personalities and predilections."

"What do they do?" I asked.

"They work on what's causing the sickness. They also work on their own spiritual evolution through serving those of us still here in the physical realm," Josie said.

I looked into the black, velvety night sky. The Southern Cross seemed to be crashing into the Earth. The mosquitoes had simmered down. Josie and I went to bed.

It was two days before I saw the entity—as João was called when he was possessed. I lined up with hundreds of others waiting to see him.

"What do you want?" the entity asked, his voice a distant but warm, low hum.

I fell on my knees blurting out, "I want a physical operation on my blind eye. I want to see. I want my spiritual eyes opened." I began to cry. João, expressionless, whispered to his attendant.

"Yes," the entity said. "Come tomorrow morning for your surgery." He scribbled on a piece of paper, handed it to his attendant, who handed it to me. I was told to move on.

I hadn't wanted surgery on my eye, but in his presence the opposite thought came out of my mouth. It was as if my subconscious had expressed my true wish. I hadn't seen the color of his eyes because of my emotional state. I was breathless, in sobs.

WHISTLING DIXIE

The next morning I walked over to the casa at 7:30. As I waited outside the main building a modern, shiny, black car with tinted windows—an anomaly in this retro-world—arrived. People gasped. João and his driver stepped out. João was tall and solidly built. His eyes were blue, his hair long and tussled. He seemed mysterious, or maybe it was the secrecy and seclusion, or the protective handlers that made him appear so. His staff closed in and herded him into a side door of the casa. I was early for the 8 a.m. session.

I waited in the main hall of the casa. I was dressed in whites, a flowing gossamer-like cotton dress that reached to the floor. It was unusual for me, but João had asked this of all who entered. People wore white T-shirts, white caftans, white shorts, white leotards, white dresses, white suits, white shirts with white pants, white scarves, white tunics, white capris. There must have been three hundred people already waiting for him—Brazilians, Indians, Americans, Europeans, Asians, people of all skin colors and social strata. Some were blind and moved with canes. Some were humpback. Some crawled. Some shook. Schizophrenics babbled. The paralyzed or partially paralyzed were lined up in wheelchairs against a sidewall. The place was filled with physical suffering and the mental anguish of patients and family members. I began weeping softly as an Asian man passed, his child pressed against his chest. The boy, thrashing uncontrollably, was trying to relieve his pain by turning

himself toward the father. The father's misery mirrored his boy's ago-
nized face. My heart flowed over with love for them. And for an instant
I felt as if I was my true self. Then the instant was over, and fear flew
back into me.

I felt utterly vulnerable. I was waiting for João, John of God, to
operate on my eye. I would be cut into without anesthesia, without
antiseptics, outside of a hospital setting, by a man who had no license
to perform surgery. I'd watched him make an incision several inches
long on a woman's stomach the day before. She'd stood relaxed, eyes
open, dazed but conscious. I'd been horrified when João stuck his first
three fingers under a flap of skin, wiggled them around, stretched, and
pulled, removing what was purported to be diseased tissue. He didn't
seem to be consciously controlling the procedure or desiring something
specific to happen to the woman. He was looking off in another direction. Someone else—some entity—was in charge. Two stitches closed
the six-inch-long cut; there were a few drops of blood on her belly.
During the procedure my body trembled; someone on the other side of
the room fainted. This had been hard to watch.

I couldn't imagine seeing out of my eye again, although the temptation to believe was strong. I'd been through so many surgeries before, I
wondered if I could bear to go through it again, I wondered if I would
feel him cutting into my eye. The thought of being able to see from my
blind eye felt too risky to trust. Maybe others could be healed here, but
me?

João had told his audience that he didn't need to cut into people to
heal them. He cut to raise people's faith. How much faith did I have?
Did I need the operation to believe? I didn't know the answer, but I
was pushing myself in a way that felt both cruel and liberating. I was
desperate to know.

I swept my eyes over a blur of faces. I nodded to Ana, who was in
the distance. I saw a gaunt, middle-aged man with hair the color of sand
leaning against a pillar. He coughed repeatedly into a white, crumpled
handkerchief. I could smell his sweat. There was a haunted or hunted

feeling about him. We began talking. He was an American. I asked if he had been here before.

"This is my second visit. The first time I was here for two months," he said, speaking in low, comforting tones. His deliberation was painful to watch.

"This is my first time at the casa. João is going to operate on my eye. I'm beside myself with worry. Have you been operated on?" I asked.

"I was never cut in to. I had the invisible surgery. I sat on a bench in a room with about forty people. I didn't do anything. I didn't pray. I just sat there for about five minutes, then left," he said.

"Did it hurt?" I asked.

"No. It was gentle, as if I was in a light dream state. But I felt something like hands inside my chest, as if something or someone was operating on my lungs," he said. A quizzical look crossed his face as he tried to explain what was inexplicable.

"Do you have faith in João's abilities?" I asked.

"I've always been skeptical of healing claims. I'm a scientist, a nuclear physicist. I work for the government at the Los Alamos National Security Science Center in New Mexico. Or I did until recently.

"I don't believe in miracles. I don't have faith, and I'm not religious." He went on, "I don't go to church. But I've gotten better here with João. I cough less. I'm sleeping more, and I can keep food in my stomach. Six months ago I was diagnosed with stage four lung cancer, inoperable. The doctors told me to put my things in order."

"The medical profession gave up on you, and that's why you came here?" I asked.

"I had nothing to lose," he said.

Sebastiao walked onto the stage and tapped the microphone. He was the casa secretary, an ex-seminary student. The American and I turned our attention to him. Sebastiao had rosy cheeks and looked like what I imagined to be a Franciscan monk. He was short and dressed in a brown tweed suit that stretched over a protruding tummy. His slacks were pressed crisp. He had dark, wavy hair. I'd learned he was closely aligned with João and had been with him for three decades. Sebastiao welcomed the group and explained the post-op procedures: no sex for forty days, no eating hot peppers, no eggs, no bananas, no alcohol. We were then asked to hold hands and pray for Medium João's health and thank God and the entities for sending love and healing to the sick.

Then he announced, "Those having surgery please come forward." I moved closer to the stage, recalling the last time I'd gone for eye surgery in New York. I had only a local anesthetic and was conscious during the operation. I'd been told the procedure was delicate, and I had to keep perfectly still. For an hour the scalpel had descended over and over again into my eye. I had not been able to speak, unable to move, unable to beg for release. It was one of the most terrifying experiences I'd ever had.

A tremor of panic seized me as Sebastiao ushered me through a plain wooden door that had a sign reading CORRENTE, or current. His brown wingtips sounded like a pair of tack hammers on the shiny linoleum floor. My hands were damp. I hesitated then moved slowly forward. The charge in the room was hot, like before an electrical storm, and I felt it waft over my skin. There was a hissing sound in the air. A Brazilian woman was throwing guttural buzzing sounds across the room. My body trembled as if I was experiencing an earthquake.

About sixty people dressed in white, their eyes closed, open palms nestled in their laps, were seated on church pews. The room was white, austere except for a milky blue stripe along the bottom wall. It looked like an insane asylum. Paintings of saints hung above eye level, eyes turning away from suffering. A haunting tune sung by the Portuguese singer Roberto Carlos played through speakers. The song was "Luz Divina" ("Divine Light"). I was in tears as I passed into the next room and felt the escalating power where João sat and spoke to patients. To the left of him stood a four-foot-tall glowing crystal. On either side of him were tables covered in white lace. The tables held yellow roses and white candles; on one was a black Madonna statue, on the other, a white statue of the Virgin Mary. The windows were covered in filmy, light blue curtains that twitched. Ceiling fans whirred. Sebastiao led me over to Miguel, João's translator.

My heart was pounding in my throat as I came face to face with the entity. I felt sheer terror.

"Dr. Oswaldo Cruz—possessing João—will operate on your left eye," Miguel said.

The person in front of me appeared to be João, who was barefoot and dressed in a light blue shirt and white pants. His brushed-back hair covered the tops of his big ears, and he wore metal frame glasses and a metal wristwatch. But I was in the presence of Dr. Cruz. João, the man, would not remember our meeting.

The incorporation of João was fascinating, strange. The personality was distinct, brusque, and cranky. Dr. Cruz seemed to spill out from the boundaries of João's skin. He felt massive and powerful. The eyes roved inside João's head, as if from a submarine. These are not eyes born with this body, I thought. In my lightheadedness I felt as if I was meeting the Great Oz, the wizard. No. The moment felt holy, as if I was in the presence of something or someone great.

Dr. Cruz, expressionless, whispered to Miguel. The loudspeakers began playing the confederate Civil War song "Dixie." This and "Oh! Susanna" were my songs as a kid. Suddenly I was a child in Missouri inhaling the delicious fragrance of new-mown hay. White, cottony clouds puckered up along the horizon. The scene whizzed by. Then Red Daddy and I were in the shining dark, our flashlights spilling into the blackened weeds and mud. Water splashed everywhere. There was the rasping sound of insects and an odd noise of something dropping into the water. Wide-eyed, Red Daddy scrabbled for the bullfrog. Its eyes were gold. Then the vision sheared off into garish psychedelic color. I was flying above the hypnotizing flow of an oily river, rope swinging like Tarzan, hearing the *whe-cheer-cheer* whistle from a red, red cardinal. *Old times they are not forgotten. Look away, look away, look away, Dixie Land.*

I felt profound happiness, as if I'd returned to my innocence. I realized I'd been heartsick most of my life. I'd felt my true self in the presence of people filled with the Holy Spirit, shouting in God's name. The Holy Rollers. I had been living in a spiritual wilderness, I thought.

"Do the spirits know my family is from the South?" I asked Miguel. "Have you ever heard this American song before?"

"No. But the entity in charge chooses the music played during surgery," he said.

"How is it the casa has this?" I asked, utterly confused.

"I have no idea how the music came to be here. It was on the table next to João, and I was told to put it on," he answered.

Suddenly the entity rose and stuck his thumb in my blind eye. It didn't hurt as much as I thought it would. Whoosh! I was surprised by the thumb but even more surprised when I flew out of my body. My mind seemed to hover above me. My body relaxed and felt airy. The entity took my hand, soothing me, as we walked toward the main stage for surgery. I felt as if I were a small, innocent child. The hugeness of the event overwhelmed me. Hundreds of people were watching. For only a quick moment I was aware of them.

Dr. Cruz, in João's body, leaned me against the wall near the door that said CORRENTE. I felt as if I were a ripple of wind, a flitting silhouette.

Sebastiao spoke to the hundreds gathered. I would discover his words months later when viewing the videotape of my operation.

"In the past Medium João has been persecuted for healing the sick. As you may have heard, a man died in the casa yesterday. The entity had told him two weeks earlier to go home and spend his remaining days with his family, that there was nothing he could do to help him. But the man refused to leave and died here in the main hall. The police authorities will arrest João if he performs surgery today."

Sebastiao handed the microphone to Dr. Cruz, the entity.

"Medium João has no vengeance in his heart. He helps everyone in need, even the police and those who persecute him. We must protect him. We do not want him to be arrested. His lawyer is here today," the entity said. People in the main hall turned, looking for the lawyer.

"Thirty years ago at a village lakeside, a court lawyer came to take him to jail for healing people, for breaking the law. João waded into the lake thigh high and pointed to the rippling water whereupon a large fish surfaced, offering itself. 'This is for you,' João told the lawyer.

"'Anyone can do that. Come out of the water. You're still going to jail,' the lawyer replied.

"João raised his arms skyward, and the lake began to froth and tremble. Hundreds of fish surfaced. 'Are these not proof enough to you that God wants me to heal the suffering?'

"Overcome with emotion the lawyer ran to João and embraced him. Since then he has defended Medium João, representing him for thirty years. We must help João today. He must heal the people.

"Is there a doctor in the house?" Dr. Cruz asked.

A gynecologist, a man from Kansas City, Missouri, and an internist, a woman from Athens, Greece, walked onto the stage. When they were settled, Dr. Cruz came for me and sat me in a chair.

"I have no license to operate on this woman's eye, but you do. You will perform the surgery," said Dr. Cruz to the gynecologist. The doctor stood there stunned. I wanted only João to operate, but I was a mute.

"I thought you called me here to observe," the gynecologist said.

"I will be with you during the operation. Have no fear," Dr. Cruz said.

"But I'm a gynecologist. I know nothing about eye surgery. I couldn't possibly touch this woman. I don't know what to do!" Dr. Cruz consulted with the Kansas City doctor for some minutes. He finally agreed to operate.

The entity's head swiveled, and it appeared as if the person inside the skin could see through the eyes of João. The personality was tangible but somehow abstract. I couldn't understand how the spirit could be in João's body, but I strongly felt this to be true.

Dr. Cruz turned to me and said, "We will operate to bring you sight. The entities will open your spiritual eyes and help you develop your mediumistic abilities. Cover the eye you can see out of." With my good eye covered, I was virtually blind. I sensed the audience, their fear and wonder, their sweat. I heard metal scraping, knives coming off a tray.

I felt pressure on my blind eye when the entity forced it wide open. Then I felt the knife cut into my eye. I was afraid the blade would pass through my eyeball and the gelatinous interior would spill onto my face. As the operation proceeded I saw the gynecologist's arm—it was like a comic book image—a mighty, black, marble forearm radiating light. (Later I would realize that I had seen it with my blind eye.) I moaned, frightened about what was happening to my eyeball, as I felt some pain. My brain felt slippery; I couldn't hold my thoughts well. Water poured from both my eyes. Dr. Cruz kept yelling, "Harder! Get in there. Do it more forcefully." Dr. Cruz was touching me on my back and was also touching the doctor (before I shut my eyes Dr. Cruz had placed his hand on the gynecologist's shoulder). The frightened Kansas City doctor was gouging my eye. But it was as if someone else beside me was feeling the pressure. I felt disembodied.

When the operation—it seemed like an eternity but was actually only five minutes long—was over, the entity moved to another patient. Two men carried me, wilted and not in control of my legs, into the post-op room in the casa.

Two women placed me in a narrow bed and tightly encased me in white sheets. A nurse placed cool, wet bandages over each of my eyes. I hurt and tried to speak, but I was told to rest. I seemed to have no weight, no density. At the same time I felt as if God had touched me, and that absorbed pleasure satisfied me deeply and seemed to relieve my inner burdens. I sensed I was given spiritual protection. Even the throbbing and the water pouring from my eyes were in concordance with the feelings of love and gratitude I held on to. It was so intense, and yet it felt as if I were ever so slightly tethered to Earth. I wanted no intrusions into this peace, this love that was endless, selfless, eternal, independent of thought. I attempted to raise my head. My thoughts evaporated.

Two hours later, the nurses helped me out of bed and escorted me from the recovery room. The door opened into the main hall of the casa. I began to move through the crowd toward the exit. An oval light extended sixty feet or more from my body. I perceived total love, not a separation, nor the boundaries of my body. My feet were hovering above the floor. Dozens of people gathered around me. "How do you feel?" "What was it like?" I couldn't bear their questions, couldn't even bear to have them near me. I was frightened, because the world outside the recovery room felt chaotic. In that moment I felt I was more spirit than flesh. I couldn't have anyone around me.

Everything was happening quickly, but inside me time slurred until it stood still. Josie rushed over to me and hovered so that no one could touch me. She spoke gently, "Sometimes people want to help and touch those who have had an operation from João. It can be disturbing because you are in a state like purification. I explained that you are not ready to speak about your operation. They mean well, but it is not what you need right now."

I nodded my head. She understood. I couldn't attend to what was going on around me. I was in such a removed state I might have easily run into a wall. I would never make it back to my room. Josie understood; she helped me into a waiting taxi that drove me the two blocks back to the pousada.

TRAVELING WITH THE ENTITIES

I stumbled inside my room and closed the cheap floral curtains to the incoming light. I felt light-headed but also bathed in grace, as if I'd been touched by the sweetest fragrance. I fumbled around trying to remove my clothes and get into bed. A dog barking outside caused me to urgently cover my ears. It felt as if he was scrabbling inside my head. I lay on the bed and drifted in a surreal space.

That evening Josie brought a tray of food to my room. She put it down on the table. I gestured her toward the hard plastic chair beside the bed.

"Let me tell you where I am." My voice was a reedy whisper.

"Shoot," she said.

"I'm having visions. I'm awake. Asleep," I said.

"Are you all right?"

"My eye really hurts."

"Keep drinking the blessed water, the holy water from the casa. This will help," she said.

I gazed at the white linoleum floor with embossed circles and petals. I continued, my voice seemed far away, "Everything seems alive. The walls, the curtains, the doors are speaking to me. The sounds, the sights, the movements are so strident that I have to shut my eyes. But then the visions take over."

"You're in a protective space. The entities are showing you things you need to know. You will benefit by what they are trying to teach you," she said.

I nodded.

"Is there anything I can bring you before I go?" she asked. I shook my head. She shut the door, and the visions started up again.

I was in a dry terrain walking toward a white car, a Mustang. The rear wheels spun backward, caught in the dirt. I was aware of communication, telepathic, aural, I wasn't sure. I heard a voice say, "You are digging deeper into the quagmire. You need to slow down. Stop everything."

The next thing I knew I was gazing at eight luminous, white, male figures. We were in the desert, in a vast plane of sand and stone. I peered into a hole dug in the sand. Was it a grave?

"Stay in this trench," said one of the male figures. "Do not raise your head or try to put a hand outside the enclosure. We will protect you, but if any part of you, even a hair, is outside the trench, we cannot help."

"Okay. But why?" I asked.

"Things will be clear to you one day."

"I understand what you are telling me. I don't know how, but I do." Something very unusual is happening, I thought. I hadn't brought myself to this solitary place. I briefly wondered if I was on Earth. I didn't try to run away, because the men's spirits made me feel at ease. Their light guided me to trust them, and I felt as if I was in the presence of very spiritual beings. I felt as if the beaming light was love. My heart and breathing slowed.

"Climb in."

I got in and flattened myself in the dirt. The sky above was Hawaiian blue, empty, limitless. Then from the distance an almost indescribable thing came hurtling closer and closer. I watched in awe as it approached. Above me, within inches of my body was a dense, heavily pitted thing like an asteroid. It covered the blue sky, and my vision became dark to the surroundings. I became absorbed in what was before me and began seeing details as if I were a microscope focusing. The thing looked like an insect with a hard, black, shiny body. Hovering above me I could see it was a living creature, an ugly and monstrous spider. Its carapace gleamed black, shiny like patent leather. It had humped shoulder protuberances, front jaws with a claw-like fang, and locomotive legs that roamed like feelers. There was a pincer claw on the front leg. Frightened, I pressed into the ground. The spirits kept their arms, like seat belts, covering me from head to toe, four figures on each side of my prone body.

More spiders moved overhead, scanning my body, looking for a way in. They could see ahead, behind, above, and to the side, all at the same time. Their eyes were like camera eyes: the lenses were concave domes, glossy and transparent, shiny black and iridescent blue. Along crests of their searchlight eyes were grotesque hair tufts. The mandibles gnawed and chomped as the spiders soared above me.

I felt I was the size of a dust mite with microscopic vision. I must be very small, I thought, to see such close-up, miniature detail. My gaze intensified. My eyes were magnifying and capturing the striking, glistening, wet-black enamel surface of the spiders. Was this heightened perception? Or visual hallucination?

I glanced down at my feet. The spirits' hands were holding firmly in position. I was terrified, paralyzed, and conscious. Soon the menacing platoon of arachnids flew away. I sighed and began breathing regularly again. I tried to get up from the trench.

"No. Do not move."

I asked questions. "Will I be going back to Ecuador? How is my family, my daughter doing? How will living by myself be?" But the figures erected a cement wall in front of my face, telling me the future would not be disclosed.

"There are powerful tests coming. Remember we are with you. Know, in the end, you will survive. Allow us to protect you."

The spiritual experience ended. I didn't know how long I'd been in the desert. Time meant nothing. It was as if I'd been with the eight beings forever. I looked around the room, stood unsteadily, and hit the switch to turn on the overhead bulb. The room seemed as if it were in bas relief, monotone, made of cardboard. I started to write down what had transpired, trying to recollect every detail. But the light hurt my eyes. I shuffled into the bathroom, relieved myself, and looked into the mirror. My shaggy blond hair was even more unruly than ever, mashed down on one side of my head. My blind left eye was red and swollen. I couldn't see out of it, and it hurt.

Suddenly I was exhausted. I turned off the light and settled back into bed. I heard voices outside my room, people returning from dinner. Josie stopped by briefly with a dinner tray. I took it, smiled weakly, and shut the door. I wasn't hungry. As I lay in bed, feeble, dazed, I noticed my hands clutching the thin sheet covering me. It felt like sandpaper.

Was it the next day? Or was it the third day? I tried to recall the dense and flitting images bombarding me since the surgery. But the gate guarding my unconscious closed. Luckily I'd managed to write a few spare notes in my journal during the past few days. I remembered that the visitation with the eight beings and spiders seemed particularly vivid.

I rose to look out the latticed window; the breeze was faint in the room. There was a patch of dusky moonlight inside the porch, and jagged shadows laced the cement wall. Swarms of insects clustered around overhead bulbs on the patio. Crickets rasped as if their irregular chirring was coming through an amplifier. My ears burned with the high pitch. Sweat rose through my skin. I suddenly needed to lie down. It was as if someone was saying, "Lie down, or fall where you are." Images came and left, swirling in a mélange of real and unreal, although I could hardly tell the difference.

On the fourth morning it was just a beautiful, ordinary November day, Monday the 19th, 2001. The digital alarm clock by the bed read 9:57 a.m. I peered around the room. In my luggage were khaki pants, a printed shirt, and clean underclothes. I checked to make sure my passport and plane tickets were in my pocketbook. The bedside table, filled with paperbacks, creams, water bottles, and snacks, seemed not in the least bit unusual, just an uninteresting and unimpressive array of common, personal items. My white casa clothes hung on hangers in an orderly fashion, not making sounds, shivering, or dancing. Nothing was vibrating. The curtains blew lightly into the room as they would on a slightly breezy day. I looked down at my nightgown and arms. All the different parts of me seemed to have coalesced. I seemingly possessed everyday logic. *Okay. I'm back.* I thought. I hadn't left my room or seen anyone but Josie in four days.

I'd recorded several visions, and it seemed the invisible world was busy, perilous, and ecstatic. I didn't know why the spirits had taken me to these places. Had the visions been meaningless, fanciful images? Or, like the dream when the doctor came to tell me I had cancer, were these portents of the future?

I made a list:

1. I hadn't been dreaming.
2. This was a series of visitations. Not dreams. Not reveries.
3. Spirits had been in my room.
4. Impossible to prove they were real.
5. My perceptions and senses felt different from normal waking life.
6. The visions felt spiritual, from God, and incredibly loving.
7. Had what I'd experienced been honed for me, made for my spiritual progress?

After a lukewarm shower I put on my tan khakis, a pale short-sleeve shirt, and a pair of flips-flops. Pacing the small room, I smoked cigarettes, listening to the voices outside as people walked toward the casa. I almost wanted to open the door and yell *Hello,* but I was still not ready. I felt energized. But the realization sank in that I would never be the same. I had seen and heard things from a very different perspective after João had stuck his thumb in my eye.

I had separated from my body just as João claimed happened to him. I believed I'd been in a four-day mystical trance, aware of other places, other realities. I'd seen spirits, left my body, and had ecstatic visions. There were many, many visitations. It wasn't like meditation. I didn't have to do anything to instigate the otherworldly flights. I hadn't asked for these things. I hadn't known they were coming. I hadn't prompted them. I hadn't prepared for any of it.

I peeled a banana. Wrote in my journal. I began thinking that these wild spiritual experiences I'd had were a gift. A way of seeing had been given to me that I thought I might be able to continue to draw from. It was the ability to discover presences visible without the aid of my eyes. I'd once thought this kind of seeing was imaginary, or symbolic. Fantastical. Unreal. But spirits had been in the room with me, and I found myself grateful for this knowledge. I still couldn't see from my eye, but the pain had subsided.

I went to find Josie. I wanted her to help me understand what had happened to me. We sat on her porch eating chocolate and smoking. The treetops swayed in the meadow across from us. There was a faint odor of cow manure. Dry tree leaves clacked in a sudden rush of wind.

"Some of the visions I had were ecstatic, others simply intense and colorful; even my eyes hurt as if I'd been in darkness and then came into a bright light. My ears ached at the slightest sounds." I rushed on. "Touching the bedspread felt impossibly dry and irritating. I remember the smell of my pillow being too pungent, unbearable, though now it no longer smells like that to me. Ordinary objects were over-stimulating."

Words continued to bellow forth. "I felt loved, susceptible, psychic, responsive, sentient, touchy. At the same time I really couldn't move, as if I was anesthetized, and I felt as if I was off in space somewhere, not inside my own body. It seemed a little too scary, a little too powerful, a little too real at times. Was I in all these other places? Was I dreaming? I felt certain that loving spirits were with me."

"The entities seem to have taken you to places that are normally closed and invisible to us," Josie said. "This type of travel is not dreaming. I'm sure there's a reason for whatever they showed you," she said, shifting ever so slightly in her chair. Her hand went for another cigarette.

"I saw many things, Josie. Portents. Places. Visions," I said. "But my eye is still blind. The physical part didn't work. Look," I said as I bent toward her.

"It's bloodshot," she said. "But you look a lot better."

"I wonder if my sight will come gradually, over time, or if I'll wake up one day seeing perfectly." Josie explained that sometimes the healings at the casa were instantaneous, and sometimes it could take years to heal.

"There is absolutely no question in my mind," I said. "I saw things that, for most people, are unimaginable."

"We've been taught since infancy that this kind of seeing is forbidden, antisocial, or even crazy," Josie said. "During childhood a way of seeing, natural and open in children, is tamped down, suppressed. This happens to all of us, because in our culture this way of seeing is not valued. The truth is that we can experience a deeper relation to spirit, to realms other than the one we see in everyday reality."

I pulled my chair back into the shade of the porch. Direct sunlight hurt my eyes. Josie measured her words, meaning that I should listen carefully. "The eye operation expanded your sense of awareness."

"It's always about what's real and not real, isn't it?" I asked.

"Yes. And reality is not always what we assume it to be." She gave me a penetrating look.

"Would you say I was in trance for those four days?"

"Do you know the definition of trance?"

"I'd like to hear your version," I said. My skin itched with excitement, because I believed I'd been in an altered state. I firmly realized it the moment I'd voiced the word. *Trance.*

"It's a state of mind, an absorption so intense that it can cause a temporary loss of consciousness to everyday things surrounding you," Josie said. "It can be spiritual. Ecstatic. What you've expressed tells me you were most likely in an extended trance."

I wanted to know about the physical, emotional, and perceptual changes I'd experienced. She told me the senses and the emotions were heightened when a person's spirit was in other realities.

"Everything was more acute," I said. "Maybe our inner life has to do with harmonizing the relationships among the various spirits as they come to us?"

"Good. You're beginning to understand," Josie said.

I told Josie about the desert, the luminous spirit figures, and the spiders.

She cut in, dropping a match in an ashtray and taking a puff, and said exactly what was on her mind. "The spirits speak through symbolism at times. João might say, 'That person has a spider.' That's what the entities call cancer."

"I did have cancer," I said. "But I'm healed now." I blew a circle of smoke and waited.

During dinner in the pousada's dining hall I did my best to eat slowly, to enjoy the food. There was chicken, beef, and lots of vegetables to choose from. The meals were served buffet style. I noticed I'd been either ravenous or devoid of hunger.

I was at the dinner table by myself when I saw a man walk over with his dinner tray looking for an open chair. I realized it was the Kansas City gynecologist. He was in his fifties and walked with a smooth, quiet stride as if he'd been living in Abadiânia all his life. He was wearing a button-down short, sleeveless, cotton plaid shirt, glasses that slipped from his nose, and a Crocodile Dundee hat, which he removed. His hair was tamped down, brown and gray, like his eyes, which were slightly magnified in the lenses. He sat down across from me. I noticed his surgeon hands and the wedding band on his left ring finger.

"Are you the one who operated on me last Thursday?" I asked with perhaps too much vigor. He stared and wrinkled the left side of his face in what I determined was concern. He began speaking as if the task was a hardship.

"Yes. I am," he said.

"What was it like for you?" I asked, breathless with anticipation.

"I didn't want to operate," he said. "I begged João not to ask me to do such a thing. I was afraid. Then he handed me the scalpel." The doctor's face came alive with emotion. "God came through me and took my hand to operate on you."

He burst into tears. "I am nobody. He came through me. God was in me!" I reached across the table and took his hand as he cried. "I had never felt that much power and love before that moment." It felt as if we'd shared a most private matter, the chemistry of that moment united us. I didn't even know his name.

"The operation was cathartic for me too," I said. "It was as potent and as powerful as giving birth to my daughter. It was ecstatic, beyond reasoning," I said.

"I think I know what you mean," the doctor said, tears running down his face. He looked at his hands, then back at me. "I'm afraid he's going to ask me to operate again. Although a part of me hopes I never have to, another part of me wants to be with him healing every time."

He'd come to the casa out of curiosity after having read about the purported miraculous healings. He was a religious Baptist. He said he'd accepted Jesus, prayed, went to church, but his faith had been shaken since witnessing the healings.

"I'm a rigorously trained medical doctor!" he said. "I don't have a clue how these healings and surgeries are possible except by God's will."

I HAVE OPENED
YOUR EYES

I'd been at the casa two months. It seemed as if another kind of test was beginning, a spiritual test, one that I wasn't sure I could pass. I wondered if physical proof that my eyesight was restored would bring me to the spiritual understanding for which I was hoping.

When my eyes were closed I could see. When they were open I couldn't, and that caused doubt to rise up in me. My mind started to fester, refusing to believe miracles even though I'd seen them. The thing I had wanted to happen at the casa, the miraculous operation, had happened. I had the desire for faith, but at the same time it was pushing me, testing me in ways that felt uncomfortable. Faith seemed to be possible only in the trance state, where I felt a sense of the sacred, the eternal.

João raised people's faith by performing miracles. One of the most dramatic miracles I saw was when the entity commanded an eight-year-old girl who'd been confined to a wheelchair for four years to rise and walk. She tottered then freed herself from holding the armrest. Her legs seemed to be learning how to work. It was almost like watching the Frankenstein movie when the beast began to come alive. Raw and twitchy movements, the beginning of aliveness. The girl almost fell a few times but persistently lifted one heavy foot after the other, then in six or eight steps, collapsed into her mother's arms. Her parents cried, gasping with disbelief and hope. It was both agonizing and beautiful to watch. Would the girl fall and hurt herself? Would more disappointment loom were the feat not to work? Then we were all witnessing something incredible. She was walking!

I befriended a German, a multiple sclerosis patient at our pousada, who couldn't walk, feed herself, or go to the bathroom on her own. She had a full-time nurse attending her. After two months she was able to eat with utensils and get around with a walker. Then there was Valeria, the pousada owner. One afternoon she showed me a scar on her belly. The entity had removed her appendix without anesthesia, without sterilization, while she stood against the wall in the casa's main hall! Another woman in her late forties discontinued her asthma medication for the first time since she was pubescent. She didn't need it anymore. I spoke with Gerard, a Brazilian whose eyesight returned after twelve years of sitting in the casa as a medium. During the sessions healing had been taking place. The entities had told him they had to work on spiritual issues before his eye problem could be addressed. Now, apparently, not only could he see, but his night vision was that of a jaguar.

Finally there was a Jewish man in his sixties who needed a hip replacement. He'd arrived at the casa, not spiritually or faith inclined. It was a last-ditch effort before he would let the doctors in New York City replace his hip joint. "The first time I walked past the entity he told me to move on, I was healed," he stated. "At that moment my pain was gone. I wasn't there more than one second. He didn't touch me or anything. I went back to my doctors and insisted I have another MRI. My hip was perfect! I never had the operation."

There were also cases where João insisted people seek medical attention. I knew the entity suggested chemotherapy to a Brazilian woman with uterine cancer. She was told the disease had progressed at such a rate that, in her case, the casa healing would not be fast enough. João was not against Western medicine. He had his own doctors for high blood pressure, though he was very secretive about his medical condition. I knew something about his health, because the mediums would talk about him.

Some people came to Brazil and expected miracles. After João operated on my eye I expected to see in the literal sense. But suddenly I had a whole new way of seeing. That was what the healing was about for me. I couldn't physically see, though some people could after their eye operations. I understood that even though I had witnessed João physically cutting in to people, the healing itself was not visible. Healing came from a different dimension. Or what some people call God.

Still, my mind worked against faith.

In the Casa de Dom Inácio people got well. People rose from wheelchairs, inoperable tumors disappeared, the blind began to see. Miraculous healing was real. I'd seen it. I didn't know how these healings were possible though. It was vaguely amusing and strange, magnificent really, the miracles and mysterious things I'd seen. And I believed I was learning something about myself. João curing this shriveled eye was to be my mountain-moving miracle. Instead I discovered I needed to embody faith. That seemed to require a miracle!

It was time to go back to New York, to reconnect with my daughter, to sign divorce papers, and deposit alimony checks in the bank. Before I left I needed to see Medium João for my post-surgery review, or *revisão*. Shuffling on my way to the entity I felt like a child, hopeful, craving attention; questions burned inside me. I needed João's love, maybe his fatherliness. I wanted to be special to him.

"You will see one day. I have opened your spiritual eyes," the entity said.

"But when?" I asked, dismayed he was terse and wasn't looking at me. I needed contact. I needed his love to have faith. I needed to know when I would see.

"Regaining your sight is really up to you. Have faith, and you will see," the entity said.

"But, but . . ."

"Come back to the casa. I want you in Brazil."

———~~~———

I returned to the Hudson Valley, taking a cab from the train station to my home. The driver pulled up to a dark, desolate-looking house. The geraniums, pale, twisted, dry versions of their former selves, were dead.

The house was sealed up, an apparition of the past. I entered. Dark shapes of furniture appeared in an expected way. But the daily life of the house had evaporated. Miles had moved out. Lana was in an early college program in Massachusetts.

I walked into the living room, dropped my bag, and switched on a lamp. The light made its way into the kitchen. I stepped through the door and peered in. I lit a burner and put on the teakettle. I needed to reclaim home even though it was only for a couple of weeks. Soon I'd be packing my things and moving to a small bungalow in nearby Woodstock. I'd be living alone. I glanced at the clock frozen at the midday hour, the information not relevant to all that had come about. Echoes of the old household loomed. I finished my tea. After staring morosely at my luggage, I dragged it upstairs and went to sleep.

The next morning I shopped for groceries. With my cart half full, I decided I'd amassed enough for a few days. I paid, arranged the bags, and got into my car. I cranked the engine and moved slowly away from the curb. That's when I hit a pole—the accident would set me back $800. I was still spacey, probably from the current at the casa, and I would have to find a way to ground myself. I realized I didn't want to go home. The walls would close in on me.

Later that day I sat at the dining room table. The teakettle sounded like a shrill steam engine. I got up to pour myself an Earl Gray. Nina, sitting on my lap, meowed for dinner. I'd picked him up from a friend's house and was glad to see him, a living relic from the past. I petted him, rubbing my hands down his smooth tortoiseshell-colored coat. My daughter had named him the moment he was born. (All our cats had girls' names.) Taking a sip of tea I opened my journal. I read it, closed the cover, and thought about the visions. Back in the real world of banking, working, and surviving, Brazil seemed like a dream.

I was left to ponder faith. The teachings I received in Brazil had been powerful, but I felt as if I had been left to my own devices. I didn't know how to do it on my own. I thought I knew what the visions and trance meant. I supposed my spiritual path would continue on in the States. I wanted to keep studying, but I didn't know what that looked like. I didn't have plans past moving to the new place in Woodstock.

A week had passed. I'd been all through the house throwing things out, packing for the move. I was upstairs when the phone rang. I shifted the phone from shoulder to shoulder as I put on another sweater. It was Josie. We talked for five minutes, and then she asked, "Do you want to come to Brazil with me as my assistant?"

"When does your group start?"

"Late January," she said. "That leaves the main question: Are you ready to get back in the harness again?"

"Yes. Give me the details. I'll be there."

I hung up the phone and packed faster. I was going back to Brazil; I'd found my second life, my new métier, I thought.

THE CURRENT

A few weeks later I was in Abadiânia as Josie's assistant for her group of nineteen people. I organized meetings, helped people get settled in their rooms, reminded them of Casa procedure, watched for urgent health problems that needed attending to. Being in Brazil again and back at the casa gave me the opportunity to learn more about trance, possession, and healing. My whole being was searching for faith. Merging with the Divine could bring trance, maybe even possession and healing, I guessed. Maybe my left eye would be able to see again.

After our group members had their spiritual surgeries I went through the line to see the entity. I didn't know which one I would encounter. In the past I'd seen Dr. Cruz, Dr. Augusto, and José Valdivino. Maybe this would be a new entity I'd never met, I thought. My vision hadn't changed.

"Will I be able to see?" I asked.

"Go sit in my current," Medium João said, inhabited by an entity I didn't recognize. "You have work to do."

I was stymied. Why not answer my question?

"What do you mean?" I asked.

"All your questions will be answered there." I was told to move on. I tamped down my frustration at the entity's answer about my eyesight. But I was greatly surprised and honored João wanted me to sit as a medium for him during sessions. Josie told me mediums received, contributed to, and sustained healing energies. This, I was told, helped Medium João and the entities do their work. I had no reservations about doing what João asked of me. He'd told me the last time I'd seen him that I needed faith to be able to see. Well, my faith would come with my eyesight. Other people asking for healing didn't necessarily have to believe. Yet even though the eye operation didn't work the way I had hoped it would, I did have extraordinary visions. That was a gift. I'd asked for one thing and gotten another. Maybe in a sense this was even better, I thought.

I'd learned from Josie that some people drawn to João's casa were undeveloped mediums themselves. "You are probably a medium, as you are very receptive to trance," she said. "You'll learn a lot by sitting in the current. Mediums are trained there. This is where you can develop your own spiritual gifts, psychic gifts, and healing abilities."

"Explain the current to me," I said. We were sitting on Josie's porch again.

"It's difficult to describe. The current has been called a tangible force, an energy, a presence, love, a spiritual power, the creative life force, which João teaches can be intensified in every person."

"What's it like to sit there?" I pressed Josie. I knew she was honest and very spiritual. I could trust her.

"In the current you may feel love, sensations you're being worked on. You may feel emotions come up. There are a variety of things that can happen. You will probably need to integrate the experience. It's subtle, therefore easy to forget when you come out."

"Should I pray? Meditate? Will I be helping others?" I asked.

"Some people meditate. Sitting in current is the foundation of the work. You will be helping others by your presence. It's a healing room not really a meditation room.

"Ask for what you want. If you don't ask the entities for help they're unemployed. Finally, don't sit near the door. It's noisier. And don't sit in the first row. Everyone goes right through your energy field, and it can be chaotic. Also, you may feel stiff or restless during the current."

The following morning I arrived on time for a 7:45 session. I entered the first current room. This room was where people would get their first healing treatment and diagnosis before going in front of the entity at the end of the second current room. The whitewashed walls, hard benches, and church-like atmosphere were not really that much different from the cinderblock Baptist church I'd attended as a child. The first time I'd passed through the current room on my way to see João, I hadn't really noticed the religious images: pictures of Jesus, Saint Francis, Saint Ignatius, the Virgin Mary, King Solomon. Now I felt a slight trepidation at sitting down in one of the pews. There was no vengeful God here, but still I worried about the Christian overtones. I didn't want to be caught up in a cult or worship situation. I didn't want to give allegiance to another, and I didn't want to get into binding obligations. Some of the New Agers might say that I wasn't surrendering to God's will. I considered their talk bunk.

There were Brazilian women smiling as I passed, mediums who would be monitoring the session. I sat in one of the back rows. The room was already packed with one hundred people. I had never practiced meditation. I wondered if that was what I was supposed to do. I really had no idea.

Arturo, a short, compact Brazilian man wearing a blue medical jacket, dress pants, and shined brown shoes came in to speak to us before the session began. He had thick, scrubby eyebrows and wavy hair. We were meant to sit in silence. Nobody was supposed to talk in the current. We were told that we had to take it seriously, and remember that everything we did, we did for God.

"The message of the casa is God is love," Arturo said. "Love heals. Wrath and judgment are human stuff. See yourself as light, centered and adding to the current. Keep your eyes closed during the session, your hands and legs uncrossed. Opening the eyes breaks the connection with the spirits who will be working on you and through you as you sit as mediums. The entities use our physical bodies to do the work here."

I shifted on the bench ready to get on with it. The talk seemed preachy, pedantic. It wasn't over though.

"You are all mediums. Focus on your responsibilities as mediums. Give. Give. Give. Don't ask for healing for yourself; the entities are working on you anyway and already know what you are asking for. Give thanks you could walk to get here. Give thanks you can brush your teeth. Many here cannot," Arturo went on.

I settled in on the hard bench. I was pressed between two others, our shoulders touching. I fidgeted, trying to get comfortable for the four-hour sitting. As soon as the session began I felt as if the power in the room developed a deep, enveloping pulse. I shut my eyes and prayed for myself and for everyone I knew (I'd been told distance was no problem for healing to take place). Within ten minutes my neck, hip, and shoulders ached ferociously. The discomfort grew. My neck wanted to stretch. I wanted to shake my legs. Stand. The wish to move was insistent as the pain pounded, pitching through me. I felt resentful. I hated the anger that came up instantly. It seemed as if I'd been bound and gagged. Then I had the idea to ask the entities to help me. The pain settled, a little.

Lines of people from the main hall began filing through the room on their way to see the entity. The monitors recited "The Lord's Prayer" and "Ave Maria" in Portuguese. In the background irritating circus music played. As more people filtered in, the room became incredibly hot. I burst out in sweat and began to shake. I felt like a fool. I hurt. My mind chased in erratic circles, berating me for sitting as I suffered. *Why should you put up with this? It's much cooler outside. This isn't helping anyone. You don't see the point.* I couldn't surrender to the current and continued berating myself. *Brain's dead. Will's dead. You're not really supposed to be doing this. Wake up! You don't want this.* I was grumpy and angry. I wanted to scream. I kept returning to the thought that I would never come back to the current and sit like this again.

I finally decided I could "do this once." Finish what I started. After some time a quieting calm descended and only deep sobbing could be heard as the sick who'd come from the main hall passed us and continued on toward João in the second current room. Smells permeated the room: a fire being extinguished, a leather saddle, pastrami, feces, cooked food, and decaying flesh. I kept feeling suffering emanating through the room, and I was overwhelmed by the sickness. We are all dying bodies, I thought. We can't live up to our aspirations; we only have enough sense to know they exist. We only have enough sense to suffer at our lack of being able to overcome our faults. I was embarrassed at how much pain I was having. I realized that everyone who passed through the line was probably embarrassed by their suffering, embarrassed by their sickness, embarrassed and let down, because they couldn't help themselves. As people, humans, we have a tough situation.

Then something took over. I was not thinking anymore. The pains went away, or my mind didn't know about them. I went into a kind of deep sleep. My body slumped over with my hands brushing the floor. I felt anesthetized. My head lay on my stomach; I had no ability to move. I was without will, unable to control my limbs, sleepy. In some small part of my brain I wondered what was happening. "We are working on you," an entity said. I began roaming in an airy, indescribable space, transported into a peaceful, timeless void. I had the strong belief that there was a superior power with me and felt united to this great energy. The entities offered me unconditional love. That was the force, the current in the room. It felt holy and was the medicine that healed the sick. The trance was so deep, the energy swirling, that I was unaware the session had ended.

As weeks progressed I continued to sit in the current during sessions, and I found it easier to go into trance. It happened pretty quickly. All I had to do was sit down and be with the silence inside me. There were lots of distractions outside, the pop music, feet shuffling, people crying, and prayers from the room monitors. It got real, very fast. Sharp pains erupted from my body. During several sessions I felt the spirits' hands inside me. I could see the hands, which were life-like but of a milky transparency. I could feel my organs being moved, and sometimes it was painful. Spirits in human form, transparent and fuzzy looking, hovered in the room. I could see them working on people. The vision reminded me of a nineteenth-century hospital or ward. One spirit took an instrument and "drilled it" through my forehead. Liquid poured from my eyes in a steady stream, unlike tears. Thereafter my head had a purple bruise where the drilling had happened. For days I couldn't touch the sore spot. I had been told by an entity that the operation opened my spiritual sight wider. Still, I could not see from my blind eye.

After dinner one night I walked over to Josie's place. She was sitting on her porch in the dark twilight and invited me to join her. "I know that look on your face," she said. "What's up?"

I asked her about surrendering in the current. "As you give up control, you will be able to accept more energy," she explained. "This will make you a strong medium."

I told her it seemed strange to get information without a teacher and to learn from disembodied spirits.

"The more you sit there, the more you'll learn. How many hours have you been in the current?"

"Maybe ninety hours," I said. "The trances seem to be deepening. But trying to explain it, there's just nothing to get a hold of, nothing solid to work with. But I learn."

Even though it was difficult, I was now devoted to going into the current. Trance was not meditation; at least not in the way I understood what that meant. It also wasn't religious in the way I'd been brought up. There was something really sweet about it, and something very intuitive, natural. But what transpired seemed difficult to report. It seemed beyond the scope of language. During the current sessions it seemed as if I was receiving deep truths, significant revelations. I understood that the power, the charisma, and the magnetism of the current was unconditional love. Love flowed like a transmission, holy and serene.

But if you were not in trance, it could be uncomfortable sitting in the current. The physical discomfort was punctuated by the fact that you felt you were in an insulated time capsule that didn't appear to be moving. In the current we sat for two sessions three days a week with each session lasting three to four hours. I wasn't sure I liked it all the time, but that was not the point. I understood the current was a protective place where healing predominated.

Between sessions in the current room I took long walks in the countryside; I needed to be in nature. I always came out of the current spacy and had a difficult time talking afterward. Planting my feet on the ground helped me remember I was of this world, not the ethereal world of spirit.

LIFE IN ABADIÂNIA

After two weeks Josie's group left. I was almost ridiculously free; time piled up into mountains. Outside of sitting in the casa sessions, the rest of my days were taken care of casually. I walked around the streets of Abadiânia, ate lunch at a leisurely pace, sometimes talked to people who were on extended healing retreats, wrote in my journal, took lackadaisical walks, took power walks, crossed the BR60 to go to the market and the video store. Whenever I left the pousada, Gentil or Valeria would caringly ask where I was going; sometimes it was just to walk around the brick factory or go to the bodega to buy cigarettes.

The casa was nothing like the rest of Brazil. Abadiânia was established around João. There were no string bikinis here, no caipirinhas, no Samba floats. João frowned on bars. He dismissed gambling. He wanted the town clean and orderly for guests. On the other side of the BR60 highway poverty was rampant. People didn't often cross the highway divide. We were separated into two worlds: one seedy, one holy.

Outside of the casa environs the town and its vicinities were rural and undeveloped with spotty, unreliable electricity. Many in town had running water and toilets but not all. Most of the locals worked on large plantations or ranches raising cattle, horses, soybeans, and eucalyptus trees. The money they earned could barely feed their families. Taxi drivers who ferried people back and forth from the casa and pousada owners were the exception; they made more than the others. Taxi drivers charged four or five dollars to drive people the few blocks back to their pousadas after surgery, and the pousadas were constantly occupied. The casa would regularly put in requests for donations of clothes, blankets, and shoes for the local townspeople.

Aside from the fact that Abadiânia didn't merit a place on land maps, what made it different from other rural areas in Brazil was the plethora of foreigners, sick people who came in droves. Those who could afford hotels were foreigners. Foreigners were considered rich. I got the feeling that the townspeople saw us auslanders as oddities. Americans and Europeans who dressed well, ate well, and seemed to have money. We were regarded with circumspection and respect. Things were cheap, and the store owners had little to sell but were grateful to get money. In town you could buy cigarettes and ice cream with flavors like *dulce de leite* (caramel) and *maracuja* (passion fruit). Yet people in our group tended to order mint chocolate chip. The locals drank *cafezhino,* a strong coffee in miniature paper-thin cups, almost thimble size. Our group added hot water and milk to make the coffee taste closer to that from a percolator. Most of my conversations in Abadiânia were with North Americans, French, Brits, and Germans.

I was deeply involved with the sick who came for treatment at the casa. Helping others during healing crises was becoming increasingly important to me. I sat with stage four cancer patients who had questions about treatments, chemo, family matters, how the casa entities helped. Some were overwhelmed by seeing spirits in their rooms or having had a disembodied presence tap them. They had questions about the spirit world and questions about going home to deal with their diseases. I rolled people in wheelchairs, helped them eat, helped them do things they couldn't do. I advised one diabetic who'd gone into shock from mistakenly taking too much insulin. João had helped her diabetes, and she didn't understand she had to lower her dosage. There were a lot of sick people, and never a lack of people who wanted to sit down and talk to me.

Because the town was isolated I liked to take a taxi to Anápolis, a cosmopolitan city about thirty minutes away. I would write my e-mails there (Abadiânia didn't have Internet), stroll around, eat lunch at a buffet-style restaurant where they served typical Brazilian fare: *feijoada,* a simmered bean and meat dish; chicken with okra; sautéed collard greens; grilled beef; *farofa,* a toasted manioc flour mixture; roast pork; green beans; black beans; piranha; pineapple; watermelon; papaya; and passion fruit mousse. Later I'd sit in the park studded with palm trees and watch the city traffic, bicycles, lovers, office workers, truck drivers, hawkers. It felt more like I was in a foreign country. I knew I was in a foreign country in Abadiânia, but it was insulated and isolated, stripped of flavor.

I had one local friend in Abadiânia, Ana, the Brazilian whom I'd met on my first visit to the casa. We'd run into each other several times, and I began to consider her a friend. While walking through town one day I found her bent over an outdoor sink scrubbing clothes. Her house, in a neighborhood tucked into a side street, was a cream-colored, one-story, cement square. There was a small, scrubby, dusty yard, a cement washbasin, and rows of line. A large shade tree edged the property. Behind her sheets, underwear, and white dresses flapped in the dry wind. Her arms were buried in deep bluing compound and soapsuds. (She washed tourists' clothes for a living.) She was wearing a black T-shirt with a picture of Bob Marley on it, flip-flops, and a faded turquoise-blue poplin skirt. Her daughter, Tanya, whom I guessed was about nineteen, was with her. I gave Tanya some chocolate from the local bodega.

"Hey, Ana," I said. "Good to see you. It's a workday for you?"

"Hi, Margaret." She pronounced my name with a "chee" ending. Mar-gar-et-chee. Her broad smile flashed. She was down-to-earth, friendly.

"I'm just doing personal wash today."

"I'll get some sodas. I'll help. We can chat if you like."

"Yes. Let's do it."

Ana had already finished the wash by the time I returned. Tanya took her soda and went off to visit a friend. Ana and I sipped our drinks sitting on the lawn, in the shade. I asked Ana where she had learned English. She told me she took classes in Brasília and occasionally helped newly arrived Americans and Brits at the casa.

She began telling me about her life. Ana never developed a strong identification with the Catholic Church. (Brazil is more than 75 percent Catholic.) She was born one of eight children to poor shopkeepers in Belo Horizonte, the capital of Minas Gerais, located in the southeast region of Brazil. She'd married and had her first child at eighteen. Her husband came from a practicing Catholic family, the son of a neighbor. He was a machinist.

Ana was unhurried as she spoke, punctuating life episodes in simple terms.

"Back then my life was upside down," she said in her best English. "My husband drank. He didn't care about us. He didn't want to work, or he complained the pay was too low. I was taking care of the baby, cooking, and working as a housekeeper. Then I got pregnant again. We fell into debt. The crises just kept building. My husband was always angry about our life, angry when the money ran out for cachaça liquor. He ranted about me not going to church. He said I went to a form of worship he didn't like. 'Macumba. That's what it is. Those evil spirits take you over,' he would say.

"Repeatedly he demanded that I turn to the Catholic Church and made the sign of a cross over me. I didn't have practicing faith with the church. I didn't go to communion. I wasn't interested in being a good Christian with its repressive laws. I was interested in the spiritual side of things, communion with spirits that could help people. You understand?"

"I do," I said as I gently squeezed her hand in mine. We spotted two women from the casa, mediums, walking slowly down the road, their arms linked. We waved. Ana rubbed her hand down her neck and continued her story.

"I was going to a spiritual center, a congregation of Africans who helped me a lot. I still do. Anyway, when Tanya was six months old I bundled her up, got my son, and we came to Abadiânia. We didn't have any money, but I knew someone I could stay with. I worked as a cook for a while. Eventually I found good work washing clothes. I have time to watch after my children, time to go to the casa, and time to go to an African spiritual center in Goiânia."

Everything about Ana conveyed a peace within her. She made a conspiratorial gesture for me to bend in closer to her. "I washed clothes for a ceremony I'm going to tomorrow night."

"You did? It's at night?"

"Yes. I'm going to an Umbanda ceremony."

She paused and looked at me carefully. She was on the verge of changing the subject, and then she continued, "It's good. It's good. It's a Yoruba religion that came with the slave trade. I've practiced with them since I was a young girl. I still do."

"They wear white clothes too?" I was befuddled. That wasn't the first question on my mind, but it was the one that popped from my mouth.

"The women wear white, long dresses, and we cover our heads in white scarves."

"What do you do in Umbanda?"

"During worship the mediums, I am one of them, are possessed by African spirits, Orixás. We incorporate spirits to heal members of the community."

"Is it like what João does?"

"It's similar to João's work in that the spirit inside the person does the healing. But one of the differences is that in Umbanda mediums are possessed and totally taken over by the spirits."

"Are the spirits the same as the ones at the casa?"

"No. They are mostly African deities. There are other spirits that heal too."

Quickly I came to understand what this might mean. "What is it like to be possessed?" I asked.

Her face lit up. "Being with the Orixá energy inside me is a gift from God. Each time my body is possessed it raises my own spirit to a higher level of consciousness. I am fortunate and honored to be a medium."

"Is it difficult being one?"

"The spirits choose us. The biggest thing is to be able to trust and surrender to the process. All spirits depend on human mediums to come to Earth. The spirits help us, and we help them."

Hearing about African spirit possession sent a current through me. I was suddenly reminded of the white beads and the Zulu priest Credo Mutwa. "During a ceremony in New York, I once was given a Zulu necklace to hold in my hands," I said. "When I touched it, a fierce energy like electricity ran throughout my body. At that moment, just like you describe possession, I felt my spirit mingle with a great power. The power took me over, completely."

Intrigued, Ana asked questions, which I readily answered as best I could, describing in detail what had taken place.

"I will bring you to Umbanda one day if my priest, Pai, agrees," she said.

The day after our conversation I caught a bus to Anápolis and looked up information on the Orixás and Umbanda in the Internet café. I learned that African slaves arrived in Brazil five hundred years ago and brought with them powerful gods and goddesses from their native lands. As the Africans were baptized and forced to attend Roman Catholic churches, they incorporated the Catholic saints into their own pantheon.

The slaves had to reshape the old African beliefs to cope with Catholicism, exploitation, and racism. Their gods, the Orixás, had dual identities with Catholic saints. The African god Oxalá represented the sun, fertility, and Jesus Christ. Iemanjá was the feminine principle linked to the ocean and Mary, mother of Christ. In addition to the Orixás there were dead souls, lesser spirits, and ancestor spirits who were called upon. Exú, prince of the crossroads, was the intermediary between humans and the powerful Orixás.

FATHER
OF THE SAINTS

We left as the sun was setting on our way to Goiânia, the city where Pai lived. Corumba, our taxi driver, was my height, five feet and five inches, and dressed in a checkered, short-sleeve shirt that stretched over a tiny tummy. His slacks were pressed crisp. He and Ana joked in Portuguese as we drove in his compact car.

"Pai Lazaro is the priest of the Umbanda temple we're going to," Ana said. "He is known as the *pai de santo,* the father of the saints. He's a down-to-earth retired mailman. At the back of his home is the *terreiro,* or house of worship."

"What will happen tonight?" I asked.

"You will see the mediums connect with the Orixás. Possession is the focal point of the ceremony."

I asked Ana about the Orixás. She explained, "They have physical representations; they are associated with forces of nature like wind, rain, waterfalls, the ocean, rivers, pools, thunder, lightning, metal, forests, and stone. Here in Brazil, where there are many various fusions of spiritual paths—different mixtures of Catholicism, African and native Brazilian beliefs, and spiritism—the Orixás often have an association with the Catholic saints who are similar to them in nature.

"The Orixás protect and heal the community," she went on. "They have their own spokesmen who are high priests and priestesses. I am a priestess of Umbanda. I've been with Pai for years."

An hour later we were on the outskirts of the high-rise city, Goiânia. Inhabited by more than one million people, it is the capital of the state of Goiás, located off the BR60 highway in the opposite direction from Brasília. We drove through large avenues, passing antique Portuguese churches, onto residential tree-lined streets with simple houses set behind brick or iron fences. It was dark due to the lack of streetlights. Bodegas dotted the street corners with signs advertising Catholic and Pentecostal churches, beer, Fanta, Diamante Negra chocolate, and chickens for sale.

We pulled up to Pai Lazaro's house, which was in the center of a quiet side street. It seemed an ordinary, two-bedroom, one-story, brick home. We got out of the car, opened the wrought iron gate, and walked up to the porch. The air was still hot. Corumba knocked. A beefy Afro-Brazilian opened the door smoking a cigarette. He was dressed in a tank top and shorts. His eyes were large and almond shaped. The whites of his eyes were discolored, slightly yellow. This was Pai. He didn't speak English. "Welcome. Welcome," he greeted us heartily in Portuguese. He spoke with Corumba, whom I had assumed was going to participate in the ceremony. "I'll wait in the car for you," he said.

Pai asked Ana and me to be seated in the living room. He lit another cigarette. "Where is she from?"

"She's from New York," Ana said.

"Tell him I'm honored to be able to attend the ceremony tonight," I said.

"But she doesn't speak Portuguese." Pai sucked on his cigarette, stomped it out in the ashtray beside his chair, and lit another. He drank thick espresso as we talked.

"I'm pleased you have brought her to me."

I found it difficult to understand his raspy voice. It may have been due to the cigarettes. He coughed too. João smoked cigarettes and had told a friend of mine that her smoking did not harm her. Some, though, had to quit the habit he said. Pai was probably one of those people. Maybe I was too.

"*Gracias por la invitación,*" I said in Spanish, knowing that many Brazilians understood the language. He looked to Ana speaking in Portuguese, "I don't understand what she's saying." Ana translated.

A middle-aged woman walked into the room carrying an espresso pot to refill Pai's flowered china cup. Mae Ione, his wife, had her hair pulled back and tight around her face. Her chin, arms, and palms were splotched. Lack of melanin. I thought of Michael Jackson and his skin whitening due to pigmentation patches. Maybe she'd been in a fire, I thought. She was not dark like Pai, whose skin tone was tending toward dense ebony. Her eyes were soft but focused. She broke into a big smile and greeted Ana and me. We made small talk. Then I presented her with an elaborate necklace made from Amazonian seeds I'd gotten during a trip to Ecuador. She thanked me.

"Pai, it's time to dress," she said. The title *Mae,* I'd learned from Ana, meant "mother" in Portuguese; *Pai,* "father." They left to change clothes for the service. Ana went off into the other bedroom to put on her white outfit. I was already dressed in white. She had informed me earlier that I needed to be pure, which was symbolized by white. I wore a long, ruffled, white skirt that covered my legs and a white, Mexican, hand-embroidered blouse.

Left alone in the living room I noted the décor. There was an armoire, two overstuffed chairs, a small couch—which I was seated on—and several tables pushed against the walls. The place was crammed with African and Brazilian tchotchkes: a naked baby doll; an African plaster bust; plastic flowers; shells; painted plates; a copper owl; pink, shiny, metal butterflies; carved animals; bowls with string, plant matter, and dirt in them; and ashtrays. There was a portrait of an American Indian chief with a feathered headdress smoking a pipe; next to it, a picture of a Christian saint with rosary beads, palms in prayer. The room was fascinating and felt African. I'd learned on the drive here that Pai's family originated from Mozambique three hundred years ago. His birth place in Minas Gerais was home to a large African population.

When Ana returned she was clad in a flowing white dress, her hair was wrapped in a strip of pristine white cloth. Long earrings dangled from her ears. "Come with me," she said. I followed her through the kitchen. A small table with a red checkered cloth held empty cups and the coffeepot with leftover syrupy contents. The room smelled of coffee and cigarettes.

We stepped down two stairs at the back of the kitchen into a narrow passageway, somewhat like a back alley. It was perpendicular to the house's backdoor, open to the night sky. The ground was dirt. There were benches, a double sink with soaps, a trash can, mops, and a pair of sneakers. This seemed like a place where people would hang out in the cool breeze and chat in the evenings.

Beyond the narrow passageway was a tin-covered enclosure where the ceremony would take place. "The alley separates the congregation from the ritual space. You will sit with them here during the ceremony," Ana said. The terreiro had open windows and a doorway through which one could watch the proceedings.

As I waited I began to reflect on my attraction to possession ceremonies. When the Holy Rollers of my youth had been possessed that energy and fervor had excited me. I realized I wanted to be bathed in that fiery, holy energy again. It felt as if things were ramping up, that I might be getting closer to learning more about possession. First there was Carlos: he was possessed by a black jaguar when he healed. Then I'd gone to João, because doctor spirits and saints possessed him. I'd been told by casa mediums that deepening trance could lead to possession. Not always, they'd said. But I hoped the three months I'd sat diligently in the casa current for João would serve me here. I realized I was on a continuum, going farther and farther to the outer reaches of awareness. My desire to be possessed by the Holy Spirit knew no bounds.

Ana arrived with other mediums from behind a hidden bend in the alley. The women wore white, flowing dresses and Yoruba-style head wraps. The men were clad in white pants and shirts. And both wore beaded necklaces that I'd been told designated their principle Orixás.

Iara, a thin, winsome young woman in her twenties, and Pai and Mae's daughter, stepped forward and hugged me. I was introduced to Zai, a six-foot, dark-skinned Brazilian who was Pai's right-hand man. When he smiled there was a space where his two upper front teeth should have been. There were five other mediums, and none of them understood Spanish, definitely not English. Ana translated minimally.

Mae arrived from the kitchen doorway wearing circular wire-rim glasses; an ankle-dusting, white, eyelet gown; and a white, frilly blouse with ropes of colorful beads draped around her neck. She also wore the necklace made from jungle seeds I'd given her. Pai was close behind her. He signaled for Ana and me to come to him.

"You can participate in the ceremony tonight," he said.

"He wants you in the room during the service," Ana said.

My eyes widened with joy. "Tell Pai how grateful I am." I wondered if I was being allowed in the ritual room because I was an American getting special treatment.

"Remove your shoes," Pai said.

"Being barefoot, you can fully connect to the earth," Ana said. "Because we are the spirits' physical representatives our feet have to be bare on the ceremonial ground." I asked for clarification. Spirits could only come through mediums who were grounded, connected to the earth. Like at the casa, she explained, the subtle beings needed our bodies and the earth energies to manifest physically through a living person.

I stashed my shoes under a bench.

Ana, the other mediums, and I entered the terreiro quietly. Pai indicated I was to stand between Ana and Zai.

"Follow the hand and foot movements of the dance if you can. Try to pick up the songs, sing," Ana said.

We made a circle around the room.

In the dim light I saw that the room was lit by candles. The terreiro's ceiling was dripping with colorful flags in pinks, golds, blues, reds, and whites, in compact rows that billowed like clouds above my head. Satin streams looped down giving the temple a festive feeling. The plastered walls were painted robin's egg blue, dingy, and dented in spots. A long, twisted vine hung from the corner of the room. Crochet ropes with plastic red roses laced the wall. On the wall were a picture of Jesus with a glowing red heart and a poster of Iemanjá, a Yoruba goddess and the feminine principle that linked to the ocean and Mary, mother of Christ. She wore a crown and a diaphanous gown as she floated over pale blue ocean. I thought of the Botticcelli painting *Birth of Venus*.

Below Iemanjá stood a battery of conga drums dressed in white "skirts." A *berimbau* (a one-stringed African instrument) and rattles hung from one wall. I was pulled away from looking at a small black door behind the drums when Ana commanded my attention. "That's a *caboclo*," she said, pointing to a plaster statue of a bearded man with a cobra headband. "They are Indian warriors, native Brazilian spirits of the forest who appear in ceremony."

It was then I noticed the wall opposite Iemanjá. A massive altar stood against that wall. Flickering votives illuminated effigies of saints, pagans, and protective entities. The shelves held covered clay jars, a Virgin Mary plaster figure with tiny painted red lips, Saint George on a bucking white stallion, a silver bell, sacred stones, bottled elixirs, a stand of long knives, flags, crosses, and dozens of statues. Everything was sparkling and yet dark.

"Represented here are the Orixás," Ana said naming them: Oxalá, Iemenjá, Ogum, Oxum, Oxossi, Iansã, Xango, Obaluaye, Nanã. She pointed to another grouping of effigies. "Those statues on the second and third shelves are the caboclos, the Indian spirits I mentioned earlier, and the *pretos velhos*, spirits of old slaves who died in captivity. They are the healers in the ceremonies," Ana whispered.

The slave statues were humbly dressed with miniature beads, canes, and pipes.

Pai entered the room from the black door, partially hidden in the wall behind the congas, the door I'd noticed moments ago. "That's Exú's room. Exú opens the avenue between the world of the Orixás' spirits and Earth," said Ana. "He must always have a room in a terreiro."

Pai walked over to the altar and stood with his back to us. He was dressed in white pants and a white shirt with red geometrical designs bordering the front and sleeves, wearing beads crossing from shoulder to chest. His feet were wide and flat like meat hammers. On the ground next to him was a large, horizontal, smooth, flat stone covered with a string of pearls. Standing on the stone was a cerulean blue and silver mermaid statue. Plants, flower petals, and seashells were strewn along the ground altar. White candles burned on the floor.

Mae sat on a stool at the opposite corner from Pai. Three barefoot African drummers wearing tank tops and short pants ripped below the knees took their places behind the congas. Community members arrived and sat on the wooden benches in the passageway. Infants, children, grandparents, teenagers, mothers, and fathers had come. After getting permission from Pai, I turned on my tape recorder to record the ceremony.

On the other side of the wall the visitors' small talk began to still. The air seemed to suck up around us with vibrant expectancy. I looked at the poised drummers. In front of them a white candle burned on the floor.

Pai rang a metal bell. "The people are in need," he said. "I call to you, the all-powerful, our father, Pai Nosso, and to our mother, Nossa Senhora." He spoke of *caridade,* charity. The mediums recited Catholic prayers as Pai picked up an eight-inch-wide triple-chain censor. He swung the incense over the altar, the mediums, the drummers, and through the passageway of the community. It filled the rooms in dense smoky clouds of pungent perfumes and herbs. "Pai is banishing harmful spirits residing in the temple or hovering around newly arrived individuals," Ana whispered to me. I was the newly arrived!

Pai's basso voice resonated beyond the very walls of the temple. Suddenly the battery of drums pounded syncopated rhythms. I was against the wall swaying with the mediums. We shook our heads in unison from left to right, left to right. As the rhythmic head turning continued beads of sweat formed and dripped from my nose.

The drums signaled, changed syncopation, and sped until mind-blowing pulses reached a climax. The bell resounded again, and the musicians slowed the tempo. I would later learn from Ana that Exú had arrived and been dispatched quickly. He was the trickster, and good or bad could happen depending on his mood.

The brass bell rang. The mediums turned, facing one another's backs. We began a clockwise movement. I followed the hand and leg motions of Ana before me. Starting with both arms held back, we advanced our stiff arms forward as if thrusting machetes in both hands. Our feet shuffled in a repetitive movement as we sang *Eu tenho siete espadas para me defender. Eu tenho Ogum em minha companhia.* "I have seven swords to defend me. I have Ogum to accompany me." Pai praised Ogum, the god of war, and the dancing picked up speed.

A black man in his sixties with fiery eyes set in a wrinkled face broke from the dancers. His head bobbed rapidly. Sensing the spirit hovering, the musicians quickened the tempo. He ripped off his shirt, rolled up his pants, and jumped into the center of the circle. He cried out, words burst forth, and spirit screams rose. He jumped, snorted, and snarled. Arms rigid as if grasping swords, he marched in the center of us, smiling, shaking his head.

I realized I was seeing spirit possession. My senses felt on high alert, and I felt deep excitement inside me, almost as if something was twisting at my solar plexus. I was moving with the mediums—sweating, singing, my hands thrusting invisible swords to the pounding rhythm, following the cues, watching the spirit possession unfold. Then, just as suddenly, the spirit left him.

Mae ran to him and covered his head with a white cloth. His form seemed to crumple under the tent. Iara and Mae steadied him then led him back to the mediums.

Pai rang his bell and called out another *ponto,* "song," and the drummers reacted on command. The rhythm, the sound surge, felt like an ocean of change. My hands mimicked the pattern of the mediums in front of me. Our arms rose and the fingertips rustled as if playing the piano, then our arms tumbled down. The pattern repeated as our feet moved in unison.

Ana was suddenly in the middle of the circle spiraling, twirling. The drums picked up on the possession. It was as if she'd been thrown into the midst of a gale. She looked like an avenging goddess. She spun; her body flowed with a powerful current. Her skirt waves created wind as her feet moved swiftly back and forth producing the circle of a whirlwind or a human tornado.

I was dancing. It was almost like what I imagined a twirling dervish would feel as the body circled round and round and brought one into trance, into tune with the spirit, and into the whole experience of being alive.

Someone handed Ana a glass of water. Ana twisted, turned, and flew upward. She emerged from her twirling pattern spraying water on the mediums and me. When it ended as suddenly as it began, Ana slumped. The glass was grabbed from her hand. Mae ran over and placed a white cloth over Ana. In minutes she returned to her place with the mediums. The Orixá was gone.

The dancing got wilder, the drums hammered vicious rhythms. Another bell was rung. Another spirit arrived. People were clapping their hands, begging, yelling, screaming, praising the spirits. The heat inside the temple made me feel dizzy, and there was a hard lump in my throat as the frenzy increased. Everything was revving up fast.

And suddenly the holiness came alive in me. Shaking, I rolled to the ground, then arched and flew across the terreiro slamming against the congas. I felt a kind of pressure on my body where I hit forcefully into the concrete, some scraping. It felt like a ferocious wild beast was exploding out from an iron cage inside me.

The drummers jumped up and grabbed my arms and legs. I was vaguely aware of this. I screamed. The thrashing went on and on, but I didn't feel the physical sensation of it. I noticed the passing thought that I was going to have some very bad hurts. (In fact, the next day my bruises would erupt, big ones.)

Pai ran over. Mae was there. The mediums surrounded me. I don't know what Pai did, but the power left, vanishing as quickly as it had come. I was in shock and couldn't get my rubbery legs to move. Three men carried me over to a bench. Mae came beside me until I was more in control of my movements.

Later I became aware the tenor of the ceremony had changed. Iara was tying a white lace bonnet onto Pai's head. I watched in a kind of torpor as the mediums incorporated the pretos velhos, bent over, hobbling, walking with canes. Ana had a shawl draped over her shoulders; her eyes focused on the ground. She had her elbow on her knee and was bent over sucking a hand-rolled cigarette. A few people were brought in from the alley.

Ana's head swayed. She bit down firmly on the cigarette that hung down her lower lip. Hands materialized from the vaporous haze as she worked on a patient. The other mediums were doing their healing work on children and the old. I looked at Pai in his bonnet. He was pouring liquid into the palm of his hand. Iara touched a match to it and a blue fireball exploded. Pai moved toward a young girl with the fire cupped in his palm. Her eyes registered alarm, and she backed up, frightened. Pai took hold of her, rubbed the flame over her chest, back, and arms. He made the sign of the cross over her chest.

I shut my eyes—perhaps I slept—and when I next looked up the pretos velhos were gone. The mediums were lining up in front of Pai.

One by one they prostrated themselves at his feet. Iara led me over to Pai. My hand hovered above my lip as I considered what to do. Awkwardly, I lay flat on my belly and placed my forehead on Pai's feet. I noticed between his right big and second toe he'd secured a burning candle. There was melting, soft wax on his foot.

UMBANDA

"After the request for the Orixás to help us, the spirits come in and take over. It can look like things are out of control, but things are being taken care of," Pai said. Ana and I sat with him while he relaxed, smoked, and drank coffee in the living room. Offhandedly, he asked, "Did you like the ceremony?"

"Yes. It was very beautiful. The ceremony was a living, breathing thing," I said. He studied me with a quizzical look then broke out into a belly laugh. Our faces were illuminated by the soft glow of overhead lights. Pai took another sip of coffee. I asked him when his ancestors arrived in Brazil. He told me his lineage was from Mozambique; that his family came as slaves, workers; and that he learned the sacred drum rhythms when he was four. He'd been a priest for three decades.

"After a ceremony you must thank the Orixás. They like the good feelings from us."

He continued, "Possession is in my blood. All of my family, my people, are touched by it in one way or another. Our mothers were priestesses; our fathers were drummers for ceremonies. We are steeped in centuries of deep belief in spirits and ancestors.

"Umbanda has been and always will be my life. *Um bandu* means "one peace." One love. One joy. Umbanda is the ultimate. It is the truth. I am Umbanda. I transform when I go into ceremony even if I'm not feeling great beforehand."

Ana and I could see Pai was tired. We made arrangements for me to come the following week.

Ana was sitting in the front seat, where she always sat to prevent carsickness. She pulled out a candy, sucked on it, and asked, "Well, what did you think?"

"Possession is really, really potent," I said.

"Margaret-chee!" She laughed. "Spirit is a frightening thing to embrace. It's so powerful."

"What about what happened to me?" I asked, visibly shaken, on the edge of the car seat behind her.

"You received the spirit without control. You were an involuntary medium."

Corumba slowed down for a detour in the road. We sat silently, watching him maneuver the orange cones and sawhorses. He seemed to be listening to us but not understanding much. He rolled his window down. Fresh, cool air entered the car. From the backseat I leaned forward between the two of them, looking at Ana.

"Was it a kind of possession?" I asked.

"Yes. A light one."

My mind tried to make a connection. I wanted to know what had gotten inside me.

"There are different levels of possession," Ana explained. "Sometimes you'll feel a spirit just pass through you leaving you shaken or conscious. Or someone could drop to the ground. But these things always happen spontaneously. A seasoned medium has learned through initiation and experience how to hold that deity. Their movements are more controlled." She paused for a moment, her forehead creasing, "Was it too much for you?"

"No," I said. "I wasn't frightened. But, in some ways, I don't have much of a context for possession other than witnessing João in entity form. Well, that's not entirely true. When I was young I watched the Holy Rollers. They're something like the Pentecostals."

"What was that like?"

"They were possessed by the Holy Spirit and spoke in tongues. They rolled on the ground. It was spectacular to see such mighty energy. The possession tonight reminded me of what I experienced so many years ago in the backlands of Missouri when I was a child. I remember the moment vividly, the thrill of it. It was the joy, the high-energy crackling that captivated me back then. And it captured me tonight."

"When a person is possessed, that energy is so big. Possession is the most basic of events. Healing happens for everybody in the community, whether they're being possessed or they're in the presence of possession. I suppose you caught some of the healing that day with the Holy Rollers."

"The Afro-Brazilian culture is different from what I saw," I said. "And yet, there is something very similar. That force. That feeling of connecting to the Divine."

Even though I was tired, my mind raced. I settled into the backseat, realizing that having the gods right there in front of me had been unnerving. It seemed dangerous but extraordinary and thrilling. The feeling inside made me want more, made me want to get in deeper. But I also thought, "I have to be careful and respectful in the presence of so much energy." The Orixás are very, very powerful. I definitely knew I wanted to be a vessel for possession. And then I thought, "Wow! It's already happening. The African gods and spirits are with me on this."

I'd once read that the San Bushmen in South Africa carried out their first ceremonies more than fifty thousand years ago. They'd dance, sing, and pray. While in trance the power of Num (energy from God) came through them like a steam engine, pumping energy into their bodies. The lightning-like energy healed and spread ecstatic joy. When one of the Bushmen was possessed with this power, he or she could touch others and pass on that power, that love, the healing.

By showing up at the possession ceremony I had in some ways agreed to interact with the Divine. I didn't believe possession was a game of psychological make-believe. I'd seen it, felt it. I believed in the sacredness and in the reality of possession. I believed a possession ceremony was an ancient art form of contacting God, that this was the first religion—not really a religion but spiritual worship. My guess was that spirit possession had been forbidden during the epochs of Christianity, Judaism, and Islam. For centuries the Western world denigrated it and saw primitivism, fetishism. The religious called it devil worship.

I didn't know how Umbanda would fit into my life or where it would lead me on my spiritual path. I was hoping I'd find out more as I continued going to Pai's ceremonies. At the ceremony I felt as if I had entered a timeless, eternal realm. The force, the power that came with the Orixás was part of that too, I suspected. Suddenly I had an irresistible urge to be in ceremony.

CONSULTING THE ORACLE

A few weeks later Ana called on me at the pousada. "Pai very much wants to speak with you," she said.

Corumba drove us to Pai's house where a young, dark-skinned man opened the door. Ana told me he was part of the extended Umbanda community. I asked her about Mae. "She's at work," Ana explained.

I followed Ana through the house to the terreiro. Pai was seated on a footstool, looking down at the Iemanjá altar. "Come here *filha* [my child]," he said.

I went to him. He took my hands and looked searchingly into my face. "Bring a chair," he said to Ana. She brought one and placed it near Pai. I sat down, wondering what I was about to hear.

"Fate will remember this day. Because it is written," he said. "I will consult the Oracle so that we may determine your Orixá."

I handed over a nominal sum of money, suggested by Ana, for the divination. Pai consecrated the offering, prayed, and sang. He got up to retrieve a dark bag and a wooden tray. The tray was oval and appeared old, with a short lip around it. Pai powdered it with a chalky substance and then removed cowrie shells from a bag. He threw the shells into the tray several times, then said, "The Orixás answer questions by influencing the way the shells fall." Before each throw Pai invoked an Orixá.

"Oxum, goddess of the rivers, is your guiding deity," he pronounced. "Her attributes and energies have been with you since birth." I'd learned from Ana she was beautiful and sensuous. She liked pearls, gold, perfume, candles, white hens, honey, and cakes as offerings.

"I have been told by the Orixá to relate a specific story about Oxum. I hope you will allow me to tell it to you?"

"Yes, Pai. I want to hear it, please."

He settled onto the stool, planting his legs firmly, feet slightly spread. I believe he spoke to the gods, because I heard prayers and soft singing. Then he turned to me. Ana translated.

"There came a time, when the Earth was very young, when the Orixás decided to split power between themselves. They thought because the Lord of Heaven, Olorum, was so very far away that they could do such a thing. They believed they did not need Him. When Olorum (Olodumare in Yoruba) found out their plans, he put his whole force and fury against them. He stopped the rain from falling on Earth, and there was a terrible drought. The Orixás and humans suffered. The earth, the animals, and the people began to die. Understanding that what they did was wrong, the Orixás wanted to plead for Olorum's forgiveness, but they didn't know how to reach heaven. Oxum said she would fly there and beg God to help them. She transformed into a beautiful peacock. But all the Orixás laughed at her. They knew it was dangerous, impossible to reach God. Determined, Oxum flew upward toward the sun. She flew higher and higher until the heat and light burned her feathers away. Her body turned black, and her head became bald. Through sheer will and determination she kept going. She had to save Earth and its people.

"Eventually she reached heaven. When Olorum saw her burned form he took pity on her and gave her water, food, and medicine. He asked, 'Why do you make this long, perilous journey?'

"She replied, 'When you, oh Lord, withheld the rain my children began to die. I came to save the Earth and my people.' The lord of heaven looked down toward Earth and knew what she said was true.

Olorum turned to Oxum, who now looked like a vulture. Looking deeply into her heart he saw great purity and goodness in her. He was so moved he announced from that day forth she would become known as the Messenger of the House of Olorum.

"Oxum, as a vulture, traveled back to Earth. With her she brought nourishing rain. To this day, whenever a person becomes a priest or priestess, before they are able to gain possession of their Orixá they must travel upriver to receive the blessings of Oxum."

"How does the parable relate to me?" I asked.

"You too reach for the heavens. You have her great determination and strength," he said. His tone became serious. "Oxum reigns over love, maternity, and marriage. The Orixás have wisdom we lack, and we must go to them for advice. People who are too materialistic, they're not in tune with the spirits. But you are. Ana has told me that you are going through divorce."

"Yes. That is true. I'm with another man now." I explained to Pai. "Can you tell me how things will work out with him?" I asked.

Pai threw the shells again and again, then he said, "This man that is not your husband, nothing good will come of it." I tried to interrupt to explain who I wanted and why, but he continued on. "Your husband is a good man. The Orixá tells me that you have been together for a long time. Your marriage could still work. You can be back together with him. The Orixás will unite you. It can be done. Would you like me to work on that?"

"I don't know," I said, surprised at the possibility of such a thing. "Maybe it's better to let things unfold naturally." Suddenly I realized that Pai was offering me magic, a spell, a love potion. I winced at the thought of my husband and all we'd been through. It hurt to think about him. Should I have Pai fix this? I wondered.

"I can help you get back together with your husband. But not with the other man. The Orixás emphatically said 'no.'"

"Oh. So that is how it is?" I said. As I sat thinking, Pai began putting away his divination things in dark cloth bags.

He looked up. "You are suffering from spiritual assault," Pai said. I was surprised at his pronouncement. Did I want help? We stood up and walked to the center of the terreiro. Pai lit candles that had been placed on the floor. I noticed an intricate ceremonial drawing on the ground made from white powder. Looking at the curlicues and lines I tried to make sense of it. The illustration was around two feet in circumference, beautifully drawn, and felt potent, symbolic. The drawing, Ana said, acted as a beacon to an Orixá. Each Orixá had his or her own symbol. Pai would not tell me who had been called.

He took a powdery substance and drew a six-foot-long, thick, black line on the floor. As he prayed to alleviate sorrow and clear the way to new hope, clear the way for peace, he had me spread my legs and straddle the line. Then Pai was behind me conversing with the spirits. I wanted to turn, to see what he was doing, but I was told to stand very still. I heard a sizzling sound. Fire raced along the black line between my legs. Sparks shot up. It was as if a musket ball had been shot between my legs. My heart hammered inside me. The sulfur smell and smoke caused me to choke.

"It is quicker to drive off evil spirits by lighting gunpowder," Ana said.

Pai passed branches and herbs over my chest and back. I was told to keep my eyes shut while he chanted over me. Then he relaxed. I opened my eyes. Pai stood there smiling. I'd been cleansed.

"It's time to leave now," Ana said. She took me to the kitchen door and walked me through the house. "Pai couldn't rest until he told you who your Orixá was. He knew about your impending divorce and wanted to help. Then there was the sticky substances, spirits causing trouble, attached to you. He dispatched them."

The next day Ana and I sat on plastic chairs comfortably padded with soft cushions in the pousada's dining room after dinner. In her flowered muslin dress and straw hat she looked like someone from the nineteenth century. She brushed her hat back, and her hair fizzed out around her head. One side of the rectangular dining room was open to the court-yard. A gentle breeze wafted through the open patio doors. The sun set as we sat with our hands around teacups. Crickets' strident cadences surrounded us. I was comforted being close to Ana. I asked her to tell me more about Umbanda. I wanted to learn, and for her to teach me, the Orixás' songs.

Ana motioned for me to move my chair closer to hers. "Umbanda honors the ancestors and contacts the forces of nature," she said. "We contact God by way of possession."

I sipped my tea as Ana told me that Umbanda practitioners believed in one God named Olorum. Under Olorum was the pantheon of spiritual Orixás, or personifications of God. The Orixás were associated with forces of nature, forces that existed within God. They were archetypal powers, part of a vast cosmology.

"Long ago the Orixás lived in Africa," Ana said. "They were all specialists in hunting, love, divination, and so on. There is Osanyin, god of the forest; Oxum, goddess of the river; and the god of fire, Xango. Each Orixá is also identified with a human effort. Xango, for instance, the Orixá who controls fire, thunder, and lightning, is also the embodiment of passion and virility. Oxum, as you know, is the goddess of sweet river water. She is love and beauty and represents all emotions and deep feelings. All natural phenomena and all everyday life occurrences are under the direct influence of the deities."

"If Oxum is my personal Orixá, how can she help me?" I asked.

"Everyone has been chosen by the Orixás before birth. You are the daughter of Oxum. Aligning with her will provide you with a more fortunate destiny. You can invoke her to help you."

I wanted to know how to communicate with Oxum.

"Through prayer, dancing, singing, sacrifice, and offerings," Ana said. "If you make an offering at the riverbank to Oxum, you would be offering a gift to the spirit of the river, because God left this power in the river."

I asked Ana about Olorum, his attributes.

"God is everything. He is a combination of polarities. The polarity consists of two forces, the force that builds up and the force that tears down. The polarities are within the Orixás too and form balance. There's no good and bad, just the two forces of creation and destruction. That is God."

TRUTH SHOT
THROUGH ME

Ana and I spent the day in session at the casa, ate quickly, and hopped into Corumba's taxi for the hour-long drive to Pai's. I'd been going to Umbanda every Wednesday for several months.

In Pai's living room I waited for everyone to dress. Ana and I then went to the alley behind the house and sat on a bench, where the mediums and community were already in place. Pai crossed in front of us, went into the terreiro, and entered the black door behind the congas. We talked among ourselves, not knowing what was about to happen. Zai was called into the room, Exú's room. We all heard explosive laughter coming from behind the wall. Zai returned a few minutes later. One by one the mediums were called in. For an audience? I wondered. All but one of them made strange sounds that penetrated into the terreiro. Then Iara called me into the grotto-like room off the terreiro—the private sanctum behind the black door.

I went in alone, a bit fearful, just as the other mediums had gone in one by one before me. I wondered why Exú wanted me. Inside he was wearing a red satin cape and held a trident, horns settled on his head. He was seated on a throne. His feverish eyes seemed to be suspended in a shiny, bright substance. It was Pai, but definitely not Pai who was speaking to me. I stood before him.

Without warning the atmosphere inside my skin tensed, crackling. I was shot through with power, as if a bolt of electricity had passed into me. My knees jumped and shook; I seized, gripped by someone brutally strong. A powerful male energy penetrated me, my boundary. The boundary of my flesh. My organs. My limbs. My brain. This wasn't a conjunction of two souls but the overpowering control of a divine presence over me. I could do nothing but observe. Without assenting, I had become a human vessel to this other.

My body, broad-shouldered and energized, whipped around on pillared legs. It was as if a flying hot weapon wielded my body, and then a rough masculine voice surprised me. His speech style, threatening and baritone like James Earl Jones, ripped through my vocal cords. The fiery sexual energy I felt inside me was irresistible, heightened to a point that felt carnivalesque. But I, Margaret, had no control, and, like a drunk, felt no embarrassment for the things he did.

The spirit was considering me; somehow I knew this. I felt his compassion, and then he howled, permeating me with ecstatic joy. He shouted and strutted, exciting and amplifying the electric energy. And then he stopped, crossed his arms over his chest, and broke into a mighty Mr. Clean smile. I was in ecstasy, but it was Exú's ecstasy.

"You are a medium," thundered Exú from Pai's body. "You should be initiated."

It was strange to feel Exú in me and know he was in Pai at the same time. I had learned that an Orixá's power was so great that it could inhabit several people at the same time and that no one person could accept more than a tiny spark of the Orixá, because the force was too strong for the human body.

And then Exú had extracted his presence from me. I was in such shock I didn't get a sense of the room. Exú told me to leave. Afterward all I could remember about the room was that the place was small, without windows.

Back in the terreiro the mediums and community members were waiting. No one spoke about what had taken place behind the small black door. All I could think of as I departed was that I had not made preparations to be possessed. I didn't know what I could have done. No one could prepare for this!

Soon Exú, in Pai's body, was swaggering into the terreiro, strutting back and forth. He smoked a cigar, laughed, and moved as if he were commandeering a stage. Exú was volatile. He hissed then broke out in deafening laughter. He passed by me. I had a cautious respect for him as I would an overly generous Mafioso type. Capone. Gambino. Galante. Exú. Rather than run, although I felt like it, I stood back from his machine gun, his power, hoping he would pass quickly. He did.

He began moving his hands like a magician. He approached Zai, gave him something, and hooted. Soon he was pecking the air with his lips and strutting like a savage chicken. He giggled then rolled onto the floor. After he'd approached everyone in the terreiro he stood and shook all over. Something deflated. You could feel it in the air. Pai turned around and faced us. He was himself again.

Pai began the Umbanda ceremony as he usually did, with the incense dispersion, the prayers to Oxalá, the incorporation of the deities, and the healing from the pretos velhos. There were several glorious, lively possessions. Exú did not turn up again. I was possessed, along with the others, by gypsy spirits.

When the ceremony ended Ana went to change her clothes. I sat in the living room ruminating. While Exú possessed me my mind had seemed as if it had been a small squeak somewhere in the nether sphere. I'd known my body was doing things. I'd witnessed the possession of my flesh from a vantage point about eight feet above my left shoulder. At least that was what I thought I remembered. Somehow locality was fuzzy and difficult to pinpoint. This was clearly a detached point of view! I thought. But detachment was not quite right either, because I had been aware of the flow of Exú's engine-like power inside me. Ecstasy had filled my entire body.

Pai, now himself, entered the living room, pulled me aside, and asked me to consider undergoing the initiation to become an Umbanda priestess. I asked him what that entailed. "When you've decided, we will go over everything you'll need to know." I told him I would consider it.

When Ana and I returned to Corumba's car I asked her what would happen during an initiation ritual. She told me I would learn how to accept the spirit. Then I would learn how to control it. I'd be secluded for a week and have to provide money for offerings, ritual materials, and sacrifices. It was highly involved and costly.

"Pai will provide you with the proper guidance and the next level of learning, a process carefully orchestrated to ensure you have the correct experience at all times," she said. "Initiation will bring you closer to Oxum and make you more aware of her presence within you."

We both sat silently for several minutes. I didn't know if I would decide to be initiated. Something held me back. I didn't want to be involved in any religion in which I had to follow rules. I didn't want to follow regulations set up by pastors, priests, popes, or Mae or Pai de Santos. But I did want more information about the ceremony we'd just left. I leaned forward in the car and tapped Ana's shoulder. "What about Exú?" I asked. "Being in the room with him was like standing inside fire, as if the matter of me transformed into other."

"I really like you Margaret-chee. I believe that you are truly on a spiritual path. Wherever I see an opportunity to impart something to you, I will. Exú is the guardian and the handler of life force. You were an implement that he worked his way through," she said.

"Please explain him to me!" I said.

"He is the meeting point that puts things together and pulls them apart."

"Like the creative and destructive forces that make Olorum?"

"Yes. Exú destroys, seduces, procreates. He is drive and the transcender of rules in order to create. He guards the change that creates the new, wonderful, and unconventional. Exú is the initiator. He is primordial. He is sexuality. And he ensures fertility. He is the one who affects all things."

"But why was Pai dressed like the devil? What does that mean?"

"In Catholicism, Exú is seen as the devil, but please don't think of this as some sort of Satanic thing," Ana said. "Exú, according to the Yoruba tribe in West Africa, is a pathological trickster deity who is also the messenger of the utmost God. His function is to mediate between the Divine and humans. His perverted tricks bring his characteristics close to the Western concept of the devil, but this is a misinterpretation. Exú and Satan are two different entities. Exú is a god who overdoes things in a frightening way. He loves to test the character of mortals in his role as the servant of Olorum. His relation to the devil is that he is the spirit of temptation. As divine trickster, Exú is not evil."

"In Native American culture up north the trickster embodies a sacred role as teacher," I said. "He raises awareness of the interconnectedness between humankind, the natural world, and the spirit world."

"Exú represents the roads that we cross and the wind from the four directions that affect us," Ana said. "As prince of the crossroads, he has the power to keep us from succeeding. Exú humbles us through his trickery regarding our petty truths. He likes to have fun. He fears nothing, and there is no road he will not travel. He is perceived as dangerous or volatile but not evil. Even though Catholics equate him with the devil, he can be a provider and beneficial helper. He can be invoked as a protection from evil."

"When Exú hit me I was passive, and then I felt as if I was a hollow tube—like the body of a bamboo flute! Ana, truth shot through me like a whistle."

I hopped out of Corumba's car and scurried into my room at Catarinense. Questions gripped me. Was that really Exú? Was that mighty power I felt divine energy in the form of Exú? (I'd come to view spirits in their various arrays and personalities, including those I'd interacted with in the casa and the Amazon jungle, as emanations of the Divine or universal energy.)

With Exú have I wandered too far? Just a few feet off the path? I sat in the plastic chair, braced myself against the back, and sighed.

A powerful disembodied soul from the beyond had seized my body. I wondered what I might have looked like. I'd seen the mediums' faces tense as they became possessed during ceremony; their eyes opened wide as the irises rolled up into the eye sockets; only the whites of their eyes showed. They had a blank expression on their faces until the spirit took hold. Did I look like them?

I had felt dislocated during the possession, but now I felt good. I noticed this was different from my experiences in trance states at the casa. Coming out of trance at the casa I didn't feel the faith and expansion that was so prevalent during these possessions. But here, having given myself over to a spirit—and in a sense lost myself—I came out of the possession feeling expanded and grounded.

What gave me pause for serious consideration was that I'd have to deal with the fact that there was me and there was them. I was Self. They were Other. My self had given way to other. This separation into two parts seemed a spiritual dilemma. My worst fear was that I would disappear and become a nonentity. That was what seemed to happen during possession. I disappeared, or let go of who I thought I was. Another soul got into me, had its way.

I'd allowed myself at possession ceremonies to be overtaken. I had wanted to be possessed. But I'd wanted control over who, when, where, how long, and why. At least logically I felt I should be in control.

The reason I wanted to experience possession was because I wanted to hone my body to incorporate greater spiritual energies. Establishing divine connection was imperative at this stage in my life. To surrender, give up my self, was not what I was looking for. I was on my sacred path. I'd honed spiritual tools, worked on myself, and survived cancer. I was not going to lose my self, my identity, to another. My goal was to establish infinite presence within me. I desired to merge with a beneficial force larger than me, to awaken and connect with the infinite, the universal.

I trusted Pai and Mae, but what about other priests? Did they have special powers that would make me do things I wouldn't want to do?

I listed the immediate benefits of the possession:

1. I knew I could differentiate between what was true and what was fake and dishonest. Possession was genuine.
2. Lending my body in possession gave me an expanded, joyous sense of self.
3. I had strong spiritual ethics. In Pai's ceremonies my personal standards had not been diminished. They may have been reinforced.
4. I was continuing to let go of limited perceptions of reality, since Ecuador, since João. I was broadening my relationship to the spirit world.
5. After possessions I felt grounded, trusted myself, and wanted to continue the ceremonies.

Possession seemed to me to be a meaningful way to relate to divine energies. My affect was certainly enlivened, in tune with it. True, I'd always been a risk taker for spiritual gain. So far possession had a positive influence on me. The community who gathered around the Orixás told me the possessions had a healthy influence on them. I knew the ceremonies made me feel stronger, and I felt I was moving in the right direction. Spirit possession could not be understood rationally. Only when returning to my body did I feel the need to question allowing another to use me.

Pai had advised me that if I were to accept Oxum, she would protect and guide me. I would be developing a deep and trusting relationship with her while entering into an expanded awareness of the spirit world relative to myself. According to Pai, I would not lose my sense of self, just the opposite.

THE QUESTION OF INITIATION

The next day, after the casa session, I sat on Josie's porch, looking out onto the enchanting garden with its papaya and avocado trees. Long nose hummingbirds with black-blue iridescent feathers whizzed in onto red bougainvillea, a flowering creeper I knew was native to South America. The beauty around here was not to be believed. There was an affectionate blackbird and two black baby toucans living at Catarinense. The toucans were infantile and reclusive. But the blackbird seemed to be hungering for human companionship. I looked up and saw the pousada owner Gentil hammering forcefully at the ground. "Fer de Lance snake," Josie said. "They're quite poisonous."

"I wish he'd just remove it to the field. I don't like killing," I said.

"There are sick people around, guests. It's too dangerous to let the snakes live."

After Gentil dispensed the snake carcass in a field I filled Josie in on Umbanda, telling her about the ceremonies, the Orixás, and Exú. The blackbird landed on my head, perched over my brow, and looked down at me. He was prone to choosing someone to annoy. I swiped gently over the top of my head where he'd landed, and he flew off.

"Umbanda makes me feel so alive," I said.

The bird circled my shoulder to land once again. "The breath of the spirits feels healthy, vital, and creative. It seems to raise my life energy, even my sexual energy. It feels similar to the energy that comes from the entities."

Josie listened carefully and said, "The casa entities raise our overall energy to heal us through the vibration of love. There's vital, creative, life energy all under the auspices of Jesus Christ and the Virgin Mother."

"Love is really important in Umbanda too. I had a taste of the creative energy last night," I said, continuing with an explanation of Exú's possession of me.

"Exú is able to be used for good or bad things," Josie said. "I don't want any spirit inside me. But one of the casa entities working alongside me is different."

I noticed the blackbird waiting for me to relax my vigilance.

"Exú's primal energy can't be easily contained within our definitions of good and evil," I said. "But I find his trickster energy to be one of the more difficult energies to understand."

"How do you decide what experiences of being possessed are okay and what others aren't?" Josie asked.

"Certainly one can't make the mistake of thinking that all possessions are good," I said. "Demonic possession or with lesser spirits would not be okay. I'm not so sure Exú is bad. In the West we always want definitives. Good or bad. Hot or cold. Exú is in between. I don't believe the Orixás in Pai's ceremony are bad spirits. I've only seen good in his Umbanda."

"For Brazilians the distinction of whether Exú is good or evil doesn't really exist. It isn't an either/or situation," Josie said.

"Yes. That's true. I didn't grow up in this culture. America doesn't have a past, a long history, or ancestors. Well, Native peoples' ancestors exist, but I don't even know my ancestry, where I came from. But the attraction to possession with the gods exists in me. It almost feels like destiny calling."

"What is it that draws you to Umbanda?"

"Possession feels natural. It's a rough and powerful beauty like a great storm. When possession happens it's as if all the sound leaves your body. Expansive beauty fills you. I don't want to give it up. But I am wary of the anomalies and discontinuity possession brings." And then I said it: "I've been told I should be initiated, to become an Umbanda priestess."

"Oh, Margaret, keep your eyes open, and be cautious."

Ana had told me as an initiate I would have to enter into a close, almost familial relationship with Oxum, one that would require animal sacrifices. I welcomed the intimacy, but the idea of sacrifice held me back. But that was not the only thing. I'd been through a lot of initiations with the Shuar healer Carlos in Ecuador, with João at the casa, and others. These initiations caused important processes to begin within me that were so powerful that the spiritual learning was imprinted for life. What I didn't like was following ordained rules. Mediums carried obligations to maintain good relations with their Orixás: wear the Orixá's favorite colors, eat his or her favorite food, avoid those that he or she dislikes, say special daily prayers, and maintain an altar. There were rules about abstaining from sex during certain times, and ritual observances to keep away negative influences. I'd learned from Ana that the Orixás were concerned with the medium's conduct and would send warnings in the form of stomachaches, headaches, or more serious sicknesses until the behavior was corrected.

Ceremony was very different from obligations and rules. In sacred space there was a lot of vulnerability, which doesn't fit in our controlled world where there is fear of being lost in something not safe. But in ceremony one was free to respond spontaneously. One was free and unconcerned about safety, mostly. As it turned out, I'd never seen anyone hurt. The spirits seemed to take care of the people they inhabited. The energy was clean, massive, less about the individual and more about the collective result. It wasn't about religious rules and prescriptions. Ritual increased my awareness. I was hungry for it, starving.

I wondered what Pai and his group thought of me, the wild-haired, white-skinned blond from New York. Our physical, social, and economic differences couldn't have been greater. Most people in our Western society would feel uncomfortable pursuing possession. For Pai, his family, and community, possession was totally appropriate and had been since they were children. There was a lot of trust and respect in the congregation. Was the culture appropriate for me? I didn't know. I felt a disconnect, certainly, about following "religious orders." In a silly way, becoming a priestess seemed to be a form of renunciation. I'd have to follow priestly rules. Perhaps there was more to it.

"Should I become a medium?" I wondered out loud, knowing neither Josie nor Ana could give me the answer. "What is my real path?"

GOD'S INSTRUMENT

I'd been in Brazil for a year with short trips back to the States. I continued to serve as a medium at casa sessions three days a week. I estimated that I'd sat in the current for four hundred hours. The casa provided structure for me. I went religiously to every session, and with my developing spiritual eyes watched the entities at work. I occasionally went through the line to see the entity. My trances in the current became deeper and deeper. I had visions of the Virgin Mary surrounded by a luscious cerulean blue mantle that fell around her feet. Wheels of twenty-four-karat gold surrounded her as she touched patients and healed them.

I looked forward to Pai's Umbanda ceremonies on Wednesday nights. I was getting closer to the Orixás: I'd had more possessions, and was learning the songs and dances. I had not yet decided if I would be initiated as Oxum's priestess.

On the long weekends I traveled with Josie, who was doing research on various Brazilian spiritual paths with a possible book project on the subject in mind, or with Ana to other temples and other healers in Minas Gerais and Goiâs, learning more about Brazilian beliefs and customs. With Pai, Mae, Zai, and Ana, I visited Umbanda houses in Uberlândia and paraded in a three-day, yearly, televised festival Nossa Senhora do Rosário e São Benedito. Umbanda groups from all over Brazil danced and sang in the streets, marching toward a four-hundred-year-old slave church. I attended ceremonies at Pai de Santo, Blind Jose's temple. Blind Jose, a highly respected and intuitive Umbanda priest, had been sightless since birth. He'd told Ana and me he'd had a vision of us and expected our arrival. I participated in all-night ceremonies at the House of Naña and Oxalá (the Divine Mother and Jesus) and other Umbanda houses I didn't know the names of.

I went to Palmelo, a small town in the countryside of Goiâs, where the trees were filled with dozens of wild parrots. According to the locals living there, 80 percent of the town's inhabitants went into trance, including children, at five each afternoon to perform healings. Ana and I attended their healings. I looked in on bedridden patients who lived in town and were cared for by the mediums. In another spiritual hospital I attended sessions with another miraculous healer, a doctor working under Saint Francis's direction. In his healing temple hundreds of cots were filled with ailing patients. The rooms were the size of airplane hangars. Josie and I were taken in to the belly of his operation and sat with the trance mediums to help raise the healing energy.

One afternoon, back at the casa in Abadiânia, I was lucky to have a meeting with João in his office. He was friendly, kind, and open to my questions. I felt honored and timid in his presence. Josie translated. I asked him why he did his healing work. "My mission is to do God's work and nothing more," he said. Humble, João rarely offered demonstrations of his personal power. Publicly he was a man of few words. "I am dedicated to God and will not accept money for services. I do not want my work discredited," he went on. I'd heard that João had received large donations for the casa from kings, queens, sheiks, powerful political leaders, and actors. João accepted donations so the casa could stay afloat. He could then treat the tens of thousands of poor patients who came for treatment.

I asked him if he was conscious of himself while healing.

"No. I do not remember performing healings," he said. "I get queasy and don't like the sight of blood when I see the surgeries on video. I'm not even in my body. I don't remember a thing."

João was the *only* person possessed by his phalange of thirty-plus entities. (The casa called possession "incorporation.") The entities that incorporate in João explained that once he was no longer alive, they would never possess another human. (They say they have a powerful connection and a purpose for coming together with João.) João is known as an unconscious medium. That means he remembers nothing during incorporations. Mediums at the casa would never be possessed by one of the entities that enter João. But in the current rooms there are literally thousands of other helping doctor spirits or entities. Mediums at the casa go into trance. We can see the spirits. But we do not become possessed.

I asked João how to become a stronger medium. He told me I should put in as many hours in the current as possible. "Everything depends on you," he said. "You have to work very hard on yourself to acquire what is necessary to work in spirit. It is demanding. You must continue your work of purification. God will use you as the instrument you are."

Josie had told me earlier not to ask him about my eye. He wouldn't know about it. "Only the entity will know," she'd said. My eyesight hadn't changed. It had been more than a year since I had been treated at the casa, and the eye was still blind. When I went before the entity he never answered questions about my eye, except to say that I had to sit in the current, that I had to have faith.

The way things were handled at the casa, the protocols, were very different from those in Umbanda. Both the casa entities and the Umbanda spirits felt like they were coming from a source outside the human realm, and I had been authentically touched by both of them. But there was a difference between dead calm trances and ecstatic possessions. The casa was about closing your eyes, stilling the body, receiving pure awareness, and going deep inside to receive visions and teachings. In the mediums' room you had to sit still. But I preferred having my whole body involved, like when communing with the Divine in Umbanda.

Umbanda was contagiously energetic, like the ceremonies I'd engaged in during my time in the Ecuadorian jungle with Carlos. Possession was about music and singing and revving up the energetic pump inside you. It was a crossing over between God and flesh. Spirit and flesh. The ancestors longed for us as we longed for them. It was a spiritual party.

I had come to a point now that I realized I had to face the differences between my trance work at the casa and being a possession medium in Umbanda. I arrived at a basic conclusion: possession was the actuated presence in the human body of a supernatural being. Trance was without the presence of a spirit in the body. Whether or not a spirit entered you was the primary difference between possession and trance.

Possessed, one can lose some or all consciousness. The entering spirit's own behavior, speech, and body movements take over. In trance there are varying degrees of consciousness (including the loss of consciousness). Trance spirits can be seen, interacted with, or can take you to other dimensions, teach you things. But you do not embody them.

I realized Umbanda made me yearn for the infinite. The passionate, primal energy brought spirit into my body. After a possession I felt as if my nervous system had been adjusted. I felt relaxed, and both enervated and calmed. For me Umbanda was embodied spiritual work. The trances at the casa numbed my body and seemed to be connected only to the mind. In trance it was as if one's thoughts were unifying or expanding. Trance had nothing to do with the body except at the casa the entities needed our physicality to bring them to Earth.

Possession was about the body and the emotions. Trance, I thought, was mostly about the mind. For me the two approaches related to two different physical systems. They were two different paths toward God.

I wondered about the possibility of living amicably between these two extremes. I wanted the insights I got while sitting in the current, and I wanted the glorious ecstasy of Umbanda. I felt that the African spirits were older, primal. They sang true to the Zulu beads I'd held nine years previously. They felt as if they were part of my destiny.

BLOOD IS LIFE AND
DEATH

Pai had committed to being in charge of making offerings to fulfill
the second of three elaborate ceremonies for Exú in Pai's country home
located in Minas Gerais, a state that bordered Goiâs. The offerings to
Exú were being given because of a request made by Ana. Exú was helping her with something she deigned not to tell me about. In exchange
she was required to pay for and participate in the ceremonies Pai would
conduct in his country home.

Corumba, Ana, and I picked up Pai and Mae on Friday morning.
We were skipping a day of sessions with João to participate in Pai's
extended weekend ceremonies in the country, the preferred place to
connect with the Umbanda spirits. From Goiânia we headed down the
GO153 state roadway, passing lush vegetation and a complex mosaic of
forests, the Cerrado, high grasslands, and rocky fields. Once we got into
Minas, I lost all sense of direction as I was gaping at rushing streams in
valley bottoms.

In the late 1600s gold was discovered in Minas Gerais, which means
General Mines. Slaves had been brought in from Bahia's sugar fields to
work the mines. They came from West Africa, Angola, the Congo, and
Mozambique. Mostly Yorubas from Nigeria inhabited the Bahia state
on the coast, but thousands were brought to Minas to work the mines. I

wondered if it was during this time that Pai's family was forcibly settled in Brazil. Acknowledging the many diverse tribes concentrated in central Brazil, I began to understand the ceremonial differences I'd seen in the many Umbanda temples I'd visited. In each house the dress was different, and certain songs, prayers, and rituals were favored over others, as well as the devotion to certain Orixás.

During the six-hour trip Pai sent us into bellyaching laughter with his jokes as we fanned our arms to banish his thick cigarette smoke from the car. Mae sat in the back with Ana and me, hands in lap, already looking rested.

After several back roads and rutted dirt paths barely big enough for the car, we pulled up to a white clapboard house that seemed to be in the middle of nowhere. There was a screen on the front door, paned windows, and a ten-foot porch. It looked like a bungalow. The grass was high and brown in patches. There were butterflies and wildflowers all around. In the middle distance beyond the house stood a dark, thick forest. Mae scuttled out of the car and stretched her legs. We pulled bags and boxes from the car. Mae pointed us to the outhouse, off the back of the kitchen. There was another building—I was told it was the temple—and sheds, lean-tos, and a wooden fence that fronted the forest.

Pai led Ana and me into the bedroom we'd be sharing. He opened the shuttered windows. Brushing sweat from my forehead I immediately noticed there was no fan. We plopped our bags down on the twin beds. Pai took us through the rest of the house—a simple living room and the second bedroom—and left us in the kitchen, where Mae had begun unloading cartons of food. There was no refrigerator; the walls were unpainted. Three spatulas hung from hooks. Ana and I started cleaning and dusting. We laid things out on the white Formica table that was surrounded by orange vinyl chairs. The sound of a truck rumbling and shouting laughter brought us to the kitchen door. Zai jumped from a dusty white van filled with more boxes of things for ceremony. He ambled into the kitchen, his arms hugging a propane tank for the stove, set it down, and gave everyone a hug. Mae made coffee.

Tin cup with hot coffee in hand, I headed outside to wash pans, dishes, and utensils in an aluminum tub. Meanwhile, Pai and Zai locked themselves in the temple to prepare for the ceremony. We weren't allowed inside. That night we ate cheese sandwiches and went to bed. Ana and I dropped off into a deep slumber. She was to make offerings to Exú in the morning.

As the sun rose Mae stood in the kitchen wearing red and white striped shorts, a T-shirt, a white head tie, and sandals. She smiled as she handed me okra to slice. Food preparation for the Orixás had begun. I chopped while Mae stewed meat at the stove. Ana shelled black-eyed peas. The kitchen filled with the wonderful smell of vegetables frying and corn porridge bubbling. I was hoping for breakfast, but none was forthcoming. We cut fruit; shucked corn; sliced mango; chopped onions, green peppers, and watermelon; and unpacked cookies, cakes, and honey. Once displayed in tureens and platters the food was set outside on a long table that had been elaborately dressed in cloth and flowers. We added cachaça liquor and cigars. It looked sumptuous, a feast for the gods. We covered the food in netting, drank strong coffee, grabbed a piece of bread, and changed into our whites. We took off for the forest, Pai and Mae leading.

Pai opened the gate to the forest. We began our journey quietly, listening to the birds. We climbed hills and then traveled down a ravine. The path began to narrow as we descended into the cool forest. Pai and Mae were in the lead, followed by Ana—with a bundle in her arms—Zai, and then me. The sounds of nature gave me a profound sense of clarity. Crossing an animal trail we came to a wide-berthed tree; underneath stood burning candles. I felt the holiness of this hidden place dedicated to Ogum. Prayers were sung, then we continued on to a fast-moving stream. Ana removed her slippers and followed Pai into the water. She looked radiant stepping into the pooling water lapping the edge of the bank. When she was waist deep in the stream, Pai prayed then dunked her backward in the river. She'd brought flowers, which were offered to the river. The current sparkled, cold and fresh. Pai led Ana out of the stream, and the group continued on. Soon we were climbing a hillock beneath an arbor of long, slender vines, passing trees festooned in ribbons and candles, each of which we prayed to as they were nature's places for Orixás to reside. Food offerings had been laid at the bases of the trees. Deeper and deeper into the forest we climbed, and although it was a bright, sunny day, the forest was dim from overhanging fronds. We came to a hidden grotto naturally dug into rock face. Pai entered. After several minutes Mae told Ana and me that we should cross into Exú's cave, because Pai, incorporated as Exú, called for us.

"This is sacred territory that no one else is allowed to cross in to," she said. The portal was low, so we stooped to enter.

In the recessed interior an elaborate altar was built into the stone with hundreds of statues and scores of lit candles. Golden candlelight, velvery black depths, and blood-red-colored figurines filtered into my eyes. Statues of crimson, horned devils with tridents and tails were perched on ledges. Seductive females dressed in rich reds pressed against the devil figurines. There were pots and unguents, thick and murky. Shadows leaped, then quickly disappeared into the dark beyond. The air was old and damp, an underground eerie world. Pai was seated on an ornately carved wooden throne, possessed by Exú. He wore a crown with horns and red and black satin clothes; his demeanor was unforgiving.

Someone I didn't know arrived and said, "You will be the servants." Ana and I were handed large carving knives. What was required of me registered, and I wanted to run out of the grotto. There were two chickens—one black, one red. The black was placed in my hands. I was told I was the stand-in for Pomba Gira, Exú's consort. "Do not incorporate her," Ana said, looking stressed. I fought the possession, holding the knife, terrified. I was prodded on by someone yelling from outside, "Do it now!" Ana and I acknowledged a formless empathy for each other. Our eyes locked briefly. A woman I didn't know laid the black chicken on a stone altar. She wrapped my arms around it, and then left the grotto when I had a firm grip.

The act was anything but swift. I hacked into the throat of the black one, bemoaning my fate as executioner, wishing to be far, far away. Ana did the same with the red chicken. The knife I held was dull like a butter knife and would not cut. I became more and more distressed, then after several attempts blood spurted on the rock. The chicken's pulsing body jerked in my hands. Horrified, I watched the chicken pass, so easily, from life to death. The woman who'd given me the bird pulled the dead body from my hands, and its blood was drained into a bowl. When she was gone I was left in the grotto for moments with Exú and Ana.

I swore to myself that this was my first and last killing. The act caused me overwhelming remorse and discomfort. I felt closer to life's value, and that made me all the more sorrowful. The act brought me concretely to the knowledge that death comes to every living thing in all its terrible glory. Death sanctified life, making it holy. This thought helped to relieve some of the guilt I was feeling. I wondered how fresh blood strengthened Exú and the community.

On the way back from the cave we stopped by another stream for a ritual purification in the cold, clear water. Then we continued on to the house quietly. I went to change clothes, wondering if all who must kill an animal to survive sorrow for taking life. We must kill to live. It was repugnant to me even though I never had this thought when buying chicken in a grocery store— cut and wrapped in Styrofoam and cellophane.

"Come for lunch," Ana said, breaking into my thoughts. The ritual food that had been made for the gods, the feast we'd prepared earlier, sat on the banquet table. The Orixás had eaten, the food was blessed, and now it would feed us. There were several spicy stews, okra, cut vegetables, fruits, tomatoes, watermelon, black-eyed peas, porridge, and cakes. I was grateful to be eating. The gods were pleased, and now it was our turn to feast. We'd been eating lightly the past days, and I was quite hungry. Pai, Zai, and Ana filled their plates and sat down. I, too, was taking some of each dish when Mae rounded the kitchen door with a steaming platter of fried chicken.

"Eat, Margaret-chee, while it's hot," she said.

"Are these the chickens sacrificed this morning?" I asked. She nodded. Timidly, I chose a piece. Mae watched as I took a bite, waiting for my approval. It was the sweetest meat I had ever eaten, juicy, delicious. I thanked her. As she offered the plate to the others, I silently thanked the chicken, pledging that its life was purposeful and that the rite was honorable.

Halfway through the meal I asked Pai about sacrifice. He stopped eating, saying, *"Sangue é vida e morte."* Blood is life. Blood is death. Spirit moves in blood. His words rang in my head.

"The Orixá eats the spirit form of the food," he went on. "And then this bounty gives us life."

"And the sacrifice for Exú?" The cave had looked to me like a black magic site, as if the offering was to the devil. "Was Exú in devil form?" I asked.

"Those are not devil horns on Exú. They are ram's horns meant to symbolize sacrifice. Exú is not bad. He is the servant. Margaret-chee, sacrifice is good for the animal. It comes back in a better form. Christ was told to sacrifice a lamb, and had he done so he would not have had to be sacrificed himself."

"Why is sacrificing a live animal to Exú necessary?"

"Exú is one of the Old Ones of Africa. He's seen too much. He's seen every depravity—war, hunger, mothers weeping. He's cried for us. He's seen life and death. Can we, insignificant people in the scope of things, presume to treat him without respect?"

"As an American, sacrifice is very hard to embrace."

"We believe all depends on sacrifice. You must give something of value in order to get something of value. You must suffer pain to gain knowledge."

"I felt the suffering, the death, in a way I've never before understood," I said. "The spirit world has long been neglected by Western culture. We have forgotten and don't understand."

"This is the way of flesh. Blood carries spirit, blood is life. Death is matter moving to spirit. We too will give our lives to feed the plants and insects in the earth."

"One more thing, Pai. If we stop making sacrifices and offerings to the spirits what will happen with the Orixás?" I asked.

"They will leave us and find other mediums who will give them offerings," he said.

When lunch was over I walked with Ana over to the terreiro. Pai and Zai were covering the floor in leaves. We helped them spread the fresh greens. The room was big, gorgeous. Statues, flowers, and offerings lined the main wall, some high, others closer to the ground. Orixás, caboclos, and saint figurines were placed in a descending form, making a triangular design of beauty. Brass bowls lit with candles reflected off the statues. There was a painting of the Virgin Mary and child, both with golden halos. Lace-covered tables, a spinning wheel, canes, pale blue satin, and strands of beads enlivened the space. Mid-floor Pai had painted an eight-foot circle in reds, greens, blues, and yellows. Depicted were stars, the sun, swords, symbols, and a circular wreath-like snake. A potted plant was placed dead center. Two dozen colored glasses with flickering candles surrounded the circle, sanctifying it.

"Go get ready," Pai said. "Ceremony will begin in half an hour."

Ana and I dressed and returned to the terreiro. About twenty people were waiting for Pai to begin. He opened the ceremony. Spirits I hadn't met before in ceremony began to arrive. Notable was a caboclo in a feathered headdress who lifted a woman over his head, began running, and circled the room several times before he put her down. The ceremony lasted three hours. The possessions were strong, glorious, and people seemed happy. I was not possessed during the ritual.

Back in Abadiânia, I sat, thinking hard about sacrifice: the smell of blood, the slick sensation on my fingers, the grossness, and horror. The turmoil and images stuck with me as I unpacked my things and went to dinner. I didn't mention my trip to Josie. I wasn't sure what I would say or how she would react. Sleep came quickly that night.

The next morning I went to the Internet café in Anápolis and looked up historical references to sacrifice. Information came from compilations of factual and general knowledge I gained while investigating a variety of sources. This is what I found:

1. The act of sanctifying or dedicating an animal to a god is a religious act. Through sacrifice the giver seeks to enter into communion with a supernatural being. Many faiths encourage believers to give up something they value as a sacrifice, or to give offerings of food.

2. The Bible gives instructions for sacrifices. It records Abraham's willingness to offer his son Isaac when God asked it of him. At the last moment God allows a ram to take Isaac's place. A similar story is found in Islam with Ishmael as the intended victim. For Christians the sacrificial lamb was Jesus Christ giving himself to be killed on the cross.

3. In the Hindu religion Krishna enumerated various forms of sacrificial acts. Krishna showed us there are many ways to offer unto God and that all are legitimate and worthy. Some are more sophisticated than others, yet every step in the stair, every rung on the ladder, is important for it leads us on to higher realities.

OCCULT POWERS

I prepared for the casa session on Wednesday morning dressed in whites and walked over to Dom Inácio. The air was spitting hot; sweat ran into my clean shirt. I was about to walk into the current room. The session hadn't started when João came out with Sebastian, Arturo, and two others I'd met since practicing at the casa. João was on the main stage, unusual but not unheard of.

"I do not cure anybody," Joao said. "It's God and the good spirits who do that. I am confident in God's presence by my side. We are all children of God, and he doesn't want any of his children to get lost."

I shuffled from one foot to another then crammed myself into the main hall with hundreds of others. I felt João was just ramping up. It was always a treat when he gave teachings.

"The entities are primarily interested in the healing of our soul. When that is accomplished our physical infirmities heal," Joao said. "We should have a positive attitude, have acceptance and faith, and we must surrender our problems to the higher power. The entities are gently pushing you in a direction of change at the level of your soul."

João stepped back and huddled with Sebastian and Arturo. Moments later he was back at the microphone.

"It has come to my attention that some of you are working with Umbanda," João said. "The Orixás are powerful and terrifying spirits who take hold of the mind and body through acts of involuntary possession. Their messages are distorted because these entities are not illuminated beings, and they may knowingly trick or hurt you."

Even though he'd sent out warnings before I hadn't taken them seriously. In the past he'd talked about disembodied spirits, saints, and dead doctors helping humans at the casa, but, to him, this was different. Disembodied African spirits could do bad things. Greedy, power hungry humans could manipulate them. They used blood sacrifice and magic potions. They couldn't be trusted. I'd heard him speak about Umbanda, black magic, and witchcraft in the past. He'd said that malevolent forces existed. Only the spirits of light, the entities, should be worked with in the spirit world. I'd heard other casa mediums talk: João hated Umbanda. I'd heard, whether it was true I didn't know, that João had attended Umbanda as a young man.

My focus went back to the stage. João's voice rose. "Working with spirits other than those at the casa is incompatible with my work. No one is to work with anyone else while attending the casa sessions. That includes Umbanda. No one working with me is to leave Abadiânia until they are ready to go home," he said.

I felt prickles all over my skin. I must have turned a putrid shade of green. Oh no! He's talking about me, I thought. It sent the fear of João through my body.

Josie was standing next to me and whispered, "He's found out you and Ana have been attending Umbanda."

Sheepishly I asked, "How did João find out?"

"Miguel told me that the taxi drivers talked with the staff in the casa office, and someone told João," Josie said.

I was stunned. But I was still determined to go to Umbanda that night. I knew I was going to go against João. I didn't see much difference between João's belief in spirits and Umbanda's belief. They both accepted spiritism as a basic tenet; they both believed in one God. I was silently outraged. Pai practiced white Umbanda and only worked with spirits of light! I would not be stopped. I didn't care what João said. He was wrong to force me to choose. Even though I opposed the practice of sacrifice, I was going to go to Pai's anyway.

That night I tried to hire Corumba to take me to Pai. "Margaret-chee, I will be banished from this town if I take you," he said. "Everyone is watching to see what will happen."

I spoke to three other drivers. None of them would take me to Pai. They didn't want to lose their jobs. I was furious.

It wasn't as if João's work in itself wasn't enough for me, I just needed to follow my own path. I knew that some people could go into trance but couldn't be possessed. I could do both. I felt like I was one of the lucky ones. A lot of the casa mediums had secretly wanted to be able to do this too. It was my right to continue my spiritual studies. For me the two spiritualities enhanced one another; great healing work with João and *magia branca,* or white magic, with Pai.

I remembered the Vatican archive No. 2117, which I first learned about when I researched information about João and the Christian Church. It said: "All practices of magic or sorcery, by which one attempts to tame occult powers so as to place them at one's service and have a supernatural power over others—even if this were for the sake of restoring their health—are gravely contrary to the virtue of religion. . . . Spiritism often implies divination or magical practices; the Church for her part warns the faithful against it. Recourse to so-called traditional cures does not justify either the invocation of evil powers or the exploitation of another's credulity."

João was treating Umbanda just like the Catholic Church treated him.

I hoped João would relax his orders, and Ana and I would be able to go back to ceremonies. "Things will settle down. We'll be able to get back to Umbanda," Ana said.

—⁓—

I decided I'd take as long as I needed to decide if I would go through initiations with Pai. It had been more than a month since I'd attended his ceremonies. I didn't get to see Pai before I left for New York. But what I did realize was that I was being forced to choose, just as I had been forced to choose as a child: follow the religion of my family or risk commerce with the devil.

Faith and Doubt

—◊—

The self is only that which is in the process of becoming, as is art.

SØREN KIERKEGAARD

A POUND OF FLESH

October 2003

I returned to New York on a cold, gray day in October. Driving to my rented cabin in Woodstock, where I'd lived since my marriage ended, I asked myself what I was doing back here. Being home meant seeing my daughter, who was now in boarding school, but apart from the pleasure of spending time with her these times spent in the States seemed fallow. I knew such time was necessary to prepare the ground for growth, but I wanted to be back in South America.

I had an appointment in New York for a mammogram. Days later, in a chilly examining room, I sat in a flimsy hospital gown—tied in the front, blue flowers on white cotton, thin from bleach, wash, and wear. I was here in New York, at Beth Israel Hospital, because the surgeon wouldn't give me my results over the phone.

The doctor sat down on his swiveling stool. We were at eye level. I clutched my thin wrap, feeling vulnerable. He had my x-rays in his hand. "I'm sorry, Margaret, but we've found . . ."

The sentences slid past my ears. I was grateful I had my tape recorder with me. I felt the fear spin inward, devouring me. I had to grab hold of my rampaging senses and thoughts so that I could focus.

"You have a rare form of cancer that we don't understand," the doctor said. "The preeminent breast pathologist in the United States has viewed your slides. We're not dealing with a mass. The cells are localized but could swiftly travel throughout the body and metastasize."

"I don't understand," I said.

"Your cancer has returned. I'm sorry," he said.

"I want to see the x-ray." He showed it to me, pointing to spots and streaks.

"But, this can't be. It's in a different area than before."

"That's why we need to rush on this." He picked up my lab folder. "I'm recommending a mastectomy and reconstruction surgery. Later on we'll start you on radiation and hormone pills."

Clutching my chest, I felt myself shrivel into a ball. "But, you told me I was fine!"

"That was three years ago, Margaret. We have to deal with what is."

"What do you think my prognosis would be after the operation?" I asked. I hadn't been expecting this, or I would have brought someone with me.

"You'll be back to work in three to six weeks," the doctor said. "We have good success with this procedure. And scheduling the reconstruction at the same time would save you an operation later on."

"What happens in a mastectomy?" He described the procedure, showing me on a picture what they would take. I told him he was not to go near my lymph nodes. I'd heard from a friend who'd had the surgery that she had weird, crawly, phantom sensations months after the operation. Her arm continued to swell with fluid, and she had constant pain.

"How long will the surgery take?"

"The mastectomy is two hours, and the reconstruction will take as long or longer. He described the hospital stay, how I'd have to drain fluids with a bulb outside my body, and the pain medication and physical therapy I would need.

"Let's schedule you now for surgery," he suggested. "We don't want the cancer to become invasive."

"But I don't want a mastectomy!" I said. I felt weak, sick to my stomach.

"Give me a call after you've had a chance to think about it," he said. "Don't take too long. I can get a spot for you in surgery next week." He left closing the door behind him. I threw my clothes on and ran from the room.

On the way out of his office I saw suite after suite for specialty cancers, their names inscribed on glass doors in elegant gold lettering. Liver cancer, lung cancer, stomach cancer . . . all neatly compartmentalized. I could see inside to the waiting rooms—so many people in so much pain. I passed the doors to the operating theaters. At the very center of the complex a glass-enclosed shop displayed items geared to hide the effects of the treatments offered—wigs, hats, prosthetic breasts. I grunted with disgust.

I don't remember how I got myself home. I made it to the subway, onto the train, and then by car to Woodstock. Passing the hardware store, not two miles from my house, I almost drove the car into a ditch. I walked into the woods behind my house. I drew a deep breath from my diaphragm and wept. Initiations, trance states—what had it all added up to? I remembered Josie telling me spiders were the symbol of cancer. I realized the vision I'd had during my eye surgery with João foretold this. Those eight entities said I would survive. But what about João? And Pai? Why hadn't being with them kept me safe? I've been with these healers the past two years, I thought. Why is this happening to me?

Suddenly I had little certainty of who I was and what I could rely on. A month ago I would have considered this impossible. Now I was angry and confused. I didn't care about João's fury against Umbanda. I didn't care about an initiation. I didn't care about being possessed. I was deadened. The air felt wintery, the sky gray. I couldn't stop crying.

I walked back to my cabin, unlocked the door, and stood in the kitchen. The big-hand clock I'd purchased in Abadiânia—with portraits of João and Dom Inácio—stared at me. It was 5:17 p.m. I dropped my things on the table, took off my scarf and coat, and sat down. Except for the pattering of rain, there were no noises. And that made it real.

I wasn't comfortable in this town. On the other side of the Hudson River, where I used to live, there were people I knew. There were meadows and open vistas overlooking the river. Here, there were dark, damp, pine forests.

I decided that I would not tell people I had the problem again, at least not most people. I wasn't answering calls. I didn't want others to know. I felt that if I vocalized it, I would be naming it, giving it power. I was worried that even thinking about it energized the thing.

Finally that night I called a close friend and told her. "Oh, Margaret. What are you going to do?"

I made her promise not to tell anyone.

Over the next few days I told the few people I felt a deep obligation to, including my mother. I didn't give details and wouldn't allow anyone to give me advice. There was only my daughter left to tell, but I wanted to talk to her in person. At eighteen she was in an early college program in Massachusetts. I telephoned her, and she agreed to visit me on the weekend.

It was the first time she'd been to my new cabin. Here she is, and I'm living in this shabby place that I hate, I thought. Our family dining table was pushed against the sidewall. We passed into the bedroom, just a room you passed to get somewhere else. We stood in the room fronting the road. It was the space where I had placed my desk, computer, chairs, and TV. There were tan floral drapes my landlord's wife had hung. We walked back into the kitchen. She looked at the table and touched a few things that had come from our old home.

"Oh, I love this blue plate," she said.

"You can have it anytime," I said.

"Mom, let's bake a cake."

"Good idea," I said.

While the cake was cooling we went to the movies.

The next morning after breakfast, I told my daughter.

She said, "Oh, Mom. When are you going to have the surgery? Will you be okay?"

I told her like the last time I would be fine. I pressed closer to her, leaning in and stroking her head. Her face was blank. Maybe she was in shock. That afternoon I drove her back to school.

When I returned to Woodstock, the house felt lonely. I sat in a chair in the little office that fronted the road, listening to the cars whizzing back and forth. It took me half an hour to consolidate my thoughts. When I thought about the past I got sad: setting the breakfast table for my daughter, waiting for the school bus to arrive to take her to school, picking pumpkins, and making a Halloween costume. I missed the comfort, the familiarity. I missed the assuredness in the commonplace but pleasing moments. I wondered how I was managing now. Not well, I thought.

If you looked inside my bungalow you'd see a few things that had come from the family home. A black leather recliner. A Navajo rug. A cactus purchased fifteen years before. Not much, really. My newly purchased double Sealy mattresses were in the small room off the kitchen. Across from the bed a six-foot cherry-wood dresser stood, purchased after the separation.

That night I climbed into bed feeling as if I was sleeping with one eye open. Around three in the morning the shrews arrived. It was the first night I noticed them, but I figured they'd gotten into the cabin to escape the cold. There were at least five moles that gathered around the bed and watched me. At first I was frightened. I wondered if they were real. I found their droppings the following morning.

The next night they came again, and I named them the Mole People. Every night they showed up, making no noise, not scuttling about. They just watched. It seemed eerie. Was I part of the underground too? Was this a sign I too would soon be under the earth? In bed the blanket rose with my breathing. My thoughts collided with one another. I shifted, but the Mole People continued to stare. I waited for them to leave. They never did when I was awake. I began to think of staring down the goblins.

In the morning I threw on yesterday's clothes and went outdoors.

It was 5:00 a.m., forty degrees. The rain had gone on too long. Staring down the goblins . . . I dropped my arms at my sides. I looked at the wild rosebushes bordering the narrow path leading to my landlord's house next door. I was waiting for the next thing, to know what the next thing was.

The following days I went through the motions of everyday life, walking in darkness. My knees trembled as I fought the misery swirling through my gut. I shook like someone with a high fever. My skull pounded as I raged silently. I screamed aloud and banged my fists over and over—into the walls, into the floor. My whole body was burning up. I paced. My eyes welled in tears as I marched into the kitchen, picking up a butcher knife. I rushed to the living room. My arm rose and fell like a guillotine as I stabbed the pillows on the couch over and over again in a frenzy. I choked, screamed, and cried all at the same time. Feathers flew, and I became wilder. The next thing I knew I'd thrown down the knife. My hand cupped over my mouth. Dry sobs followed as I collapsed onto the floor.

I had not thought it would be so exhausting, this sickness, this anger, this suffering. The spider vision repeated over and over in my mind, ominous in overtone. João had opened me to the very visions that foreshadowed my cancer. It felt too ironic.

After only a few weeks I purchased a ticket to Brazil with money from my divorce settlement. I was going back to João. Even though my eye wasn't healed, I was expecting him to heal the cancer.

SPIRITUAL SURGERY

Back in Abadiânia on a Sunday afternoon in late October, I settled into the pousada in a room different from my usual one but virtually the same setup. After resting for a bit I unpacked my things and walked over to the dining hall for dinner. There I spied Josie. We sat down together. She recognized a look on my face of extreme vulnerability. I'd just come from a nap where I had been dreaming about death.

"I have cancer," I said. "João must heal me." Why did I have to keep stressing the word *cancer*? I hated the sound of it.

"Oh, Margaret. I'm so sorry. It's good you came right away. I'll help you in whatever way I can. How long are you staying?" she asked.

I said I didn't know. "Until I am healed."

On Wednesday morning I waited in the casa line to have my audience with João. When I stood in front of him I didn't get a chance to tell him about the cancer, to form my request. He looked at Miguel, handed me a script, and said, *"Operação."* I felt scared, weak. That afternoon Sebastian called for those having surgery to approach the stage. We were led into the room for invisible surgeries, seated on benches, and told to close our eyes. It was like sitting in the current but more potent. Immediately I slumped over until one of the monitors helped me up and outside. It turned out it had been only a five-minute session. But I felt as if I'd been spun around until I couldn't stand. Outside, I managed to hire a taxi to Catarinense.

I undressed, put on a casual T-shirt and loose pants, and got into bed. I was sharply aware of noises and the sound of a bird flying overhead. It fixed my attention to the point where I found I was tracking its movements inside my body. I was physically feeling its presence. I had difficulty discerning the separation between the bird and myself.

I detected movement of light from the opening door. It was early evening when Josie came in with a tray of food.

"How are you doing?" she asked.

"I feel as I did after my eye surgery two years ago," I said. "I've been afraid to open my eyes, because when I do everything in my room breathes. The curtains, the walls, the door, each have their own rhythm. It's as if I am on some kind of a drug, and I want the molecules to slow down. The frenzy causes me to close my eyes again. But when I do that I see another world. Opening my eyes again I have to watch my clothes hum on the hanger, beating a rhythm different from the walls and window. It's too much."

Josie was talking. I kept gazing at her not quite grasping what she was saying. I was still rehashing the visions.

"The walls, the windows, the doors inhale and exhale. I am overwhelmed in this sensory overload," I said.

"Margaret, you are capable of seeing the wonder of it all," Josie said. "That's a gift. You were born with that. The spirit world, as you know, is very different from our world. You see in a way that is structurally different from ordinary vision, a reality the entities are showing you," she said as she gently rubbed the back of my neck.

"I had a dream. Or a vision," I said. "The images had come in fast. A steel ship covered in corroding rust appeared, riding fierce waves on the Atlantic. The deckhands worked sanding the ship, cleaning it; they told me my cancer was being handled in the same way. It was being cleaned up."

"It sounds to me as if the entities are going to heal you." With that last thought Josie left.

I went back to sleep—until Monday. I vaguely remembered Josie coming in and out of my room.

When I was feeling better I got out of bed. I realized five days had vanished. I put on a sundress and lipstick and went out from the room. I didn't have the energy or desire to think about cancer. I felt as if I was just getting back on my feet. Later I walked to the other side of town to get the Denzel Washington film *The Hurricane* at the video store. That night, along with other pousada guests, I watched the film in the dining room.

Tuesday I sat outside my room, rested, and wrote in my journal. I looked out onto the vast panorama of tropical trees, flowers, and hummingbirds. I felt safe at the casa, more so than when I was in New York. There seemed to be hope here, promise that came with the warmth and healing sun.

On Wednesday, I returned to the casa and lined up for my revisão. Again, I couldn't get a word in before the entity said, "Operação." That afternoon I had another invisible surgery.

I returned to my room and stayed in bed until the following Monday. Just like the week before, I was off in the netherworld. The visions and physical sensations bombarded me as before. I felt frail but also swept up in the midst of torrid emotions and garish visions. Josie visited me daily, bringing trays of food. Ana visited twice when on rare occasions I sat outside my room.

"I've spoken to Pai," she said. "He says not to worry about missing Umbanda. He hopes you get well soon and is making offerings for your recovery."

"Send him and Mae my love," I said.

My third and fourth week in Abadiânia, I continued going before the entity on Wednesdays. "Operação," João said again, both times. I pleaded for news, a diagnosis, hope, advice. He wouldn't say anything about my condition even though I pressed him weekly for information. He emitted one word when I went for my review each week: "Operation." Two more weeks of lying in bed, submitting to visions and acute sensory intensity. During the month of surgeries I never went into the current, never left town, never ventured forth on nature walks. I interacted with the entities. I had no idea what was going on outside my small room.

After the fourth operation and the consecutive five days of visions, I got up from bed feeling refreshed. As usual I went to see the entity, my fifth trip through the line, or, in calendar time, five foggy weeks later. João, incorporated as Dr. Cruz, the entity who had originally operated on my eye, told me to go with Josie to the sacred waterfall for cleansing. She agreed to take me.

As I was feeling unusually strong and healthy, we decided to go early the next morning. Leaving the pousada we walked toward the casa and entered the casa grounds, passing the casa crystal shop. A narrow dirt road snaked down a steep hill. We walked toward where the hill began then descended on the path, focusing on our intention step by step. The sacred waterfall was hidden on casa property. I had the sense of being on a pilgrimage.

"One must have the permission of the entities to come to the *cachoeira,* the waterfall," Josie said. "For me, the feeling of being in this magical area is like being in a hushed, very sacred cathedral."

We entered a wooded area. The air smelled of dark, wet earth. Josie and I stood next to a tree surrounded by tiny yellow flowers. The faint breeze rustled the intricately woven branches. Josie's face was infused with stately calm. A truck and voices beyond the forest shattered the morning stillness. We silently continued and turned onto a narrow, twisting path, following it until we came to a kind of doorway made by two trees. The stillness was absolute. Morphul butterflies, iridescent blue, seemed to be floating effortlessly, like falling leaves.

"We must ask the spirits of the land for permission to enter," Josie said. We prayed at the gateway to the sacred cachoeira, hearing the sound of water splashing, true and strong. Birdsong spilled into the surroundings. Once permission was granted by the residing spirits we descended toward the water. The air had taken on a green transparency as light reflected down from the tree leaves and onto the pooling water below. We were on a short bridge made out of cut poles. Leaning over the balustrade, we rested for a moment and gazed at the cachoeira. It was cool and shadowy where we stood. Thin rays of sunlight spilled through the trees.

Arriving at the edge of the pooling water I stopped to take off my outer clothes. I waded into the cold water, trying not to slip on the mossy stones underfoot. When I reached the center of the pool and stood before the falls, I sucked in my breath and prayed before vanishing into the phosphorescent mist. Everything blurred as I braced for the impact of water. Josie had followed me in and had raised her arms toward the falls, toward me. I felt the cold, purifying energy. It seemed as if I was being highly charged and at the same time as if I was discharging burdens, shedding pain, and releasing pent-up misery from the disease. As I stepped from the waterfall I felt at peace. Josie took my hand, easing me up toward the embankment. Pieces of leaves and twigs clung to my wet legs. Josie's fingers brushed lightly over my body.

I sat and waited while Josie stood under the falls. Beaming with delight, she exited the curtain of water after a few minutes and came to where I was sitting.

"Your spirit shone bright and iridescent," she said, sitting beside me on a boulder.

I prodded a pebble with my toe. I welled up. The cachoeira seemed to release the tension that had held me mute.

"All those weeks in bed I felt as if I could live or die," I said. "There was no difference in my feelings about which would come. I didn't worry so much about cancer. I was too weak and sensitive to think."

Josie nodded, and I continued. "I came to accept that I could die. I wasn't sad or happy. The intensity of strangely feeling no judgment during the spirits' visitations was what made these weeks so unusual for me."

"You were under protection, and it was important not to dwell on the illness," she said.

"Yes. That's what the entities said to me. How this relates to my sickness, I don't know."

"You must go back to João and find out if your treatment is finished," Josie said.

As we walked back to the pousada, a triple rainbow spread across the horizon, fat and saturated with color.

The sixth week I entered the casa dressed in white as I always did. Hundreds of people were milling about. Even though many of the faces were new, the suffering was not. Sadness, pain, and weariness were everywhere. People fanned themselves, sat in wheelchairs and on benches, leaned against walls and posts, scraped along the floor on crutches. Mothers with children in their arms looked desperate. Some were quietly weeping. Sebastian came onto the stage, greeted everyone in four languages, then invited two patients who had been healed—one of multiple sclerosis and one of an inoperable brain tumor that had disappeared—to give testimony. Miracles seemed normal at the casa. But not everyone received health, I realized. When the speeches were over Sebastian called for those having surgery to come forward. I watched as several dozen people followed him into the surgery room. I waited for the revision line to be called so that I could stand before the entity.

When I reached João the entity did not move. This is what I saw: his legs were spread wide, his bare feet nestled in a white pillow. Miguel, his translator, stood like a statue. The flowers, effigies, and mediums made it seem as though time had stopped. I stood before João, fearful and confused. I felt numb, as if I was in a deep freeze.

"Do I still have cancer?" I asked in a breathless whisper. A fly whizzed past. João turned his head and looked at Miguel.

"You won't have a problem," he said, incorporated as Dr. Oswaldo Cruz. I remembered trying to understand his words and failing. Did he mean I wouldn't die? The moment was stark, outlined against an arrangement, like a pattern of fibers in wood, the grain alignment on an axis I could not comprehend.

"But should I have surgery in New York?"

"You do not need surgery," Dr. Cruz said. "There's nothing else you have to do. The cancer is taken care of."

"Is it gone?" I asked.

The entity refused to give me any more information.

I walked away, a measured relief filled me; in a heartbeat I thought, it's over. It had once seemed impossible to imagine this could be done away with. The trick was to keep the thought I was cured alive. But I wanted verifiable proof—like one gets from the Western medical establishment—that the cancer was gone. As I walked back to the pousada I questioned João's decree. He'd refused to use the words "It is gone." How could I know the invisible surgeries worked? I still couldn't see from my eye.

I was struck with the absolute fragility of my situation. I'd gone into João's world and played by his rules. I'd worn white. I'd sat as a medium and even accepted it might take years for my eye to heal. I'd witnessed amazing healings of others. I'd stopped working with Pai. (Although I didn't give up hope that I'd be able to go back to do ceremonies one day.) I'd been very open.

But I have cancer! I couldn't wait and see. I couldn't trust João! I had to know I was safe. I returned to New York.

CRISIS OF FAITH

I requested another biopsy during my appointment in the New York City hospital. I had to know if I still had cancer.

"Because you don't have a mass, another biopsy won't help. We've found cancer, and no amount of clear tissue cultures can eradicate that," the doctor said. I sat on the cold, hard examination table watching the florescent lights pulsate in a sickening throb. Everything around me felt sterile, dead. Brazil had been so different—warm, free, and hopeful. Suddenly it was as if all the faith and hope I'd ever earned ebbed and flowed from my very body.

When I'd come back from Ecuador after my first round of cancer, my New York doctors were amazed that their tests and scans showed no cancer. This time the doctor wanted to do a mastectomy and give me radiation and hormone therapy. He was basing his decision on the scans I'd had before I went to Brazil. I couldn't trust that the cancer would not metastasize. Nor did I believe João really took care of it like he said. Did I have faith? No! I felt like a complete failure and, worse, a fake.

With dread I consented to the operation—not a mastectomy but a lumpectomy. Apparently the rabid cells were grouped in one section of the breast. The doctor thought a lumpectomy might not help. "A few lone cells could migrate and invade your body. Do you want to take that chance?"

"I'll take my chances with a lumpectomy."

"It's going to be a large excision," the doctor said. "Your nipple and breast are not going to look the same. With a mastectomy and reconstruction you'd look better." He offered to have a reconstruction surgeon scheduled to perform the procedure right after the removal of my breast. Both could be done at the same time.

He asked if I could live every day with the knowledge the cancer could spread and I wouldn't know until it was too late. Did I understand the risk I was taking?

I remained firm.

I knew what was ahead—the steel, the cold harsh lights, being put under sedation, waking to pain. I told myself that I was undergoing a procedure like the extraction of a rotten tooth. Once the tooth was removed, my body would be healthy again.

I would be operated on during an outpatient surgery. Two girlfriends in whom I'd confided drove me to the city early one morning for the lumpectomy. They spent the day shopping while I was in surgery and recovery. That evening they drove me back to Upstate New York. I holed up at my girlfriend's home for five days recuperating.

A week later the surgeon called: he needed to go in again as the tissue margins weren't clear. The tissue was found to have cancer cells. "Let me perform a total mastectomy." I refused, but I agreed to let him take out another chunk. I wanted him to stay away from my chest walls, my lymph nodes, the muscles. I did not want the mastectomy.

I went into surgery again, and then recuperated. It was December when I returned to my home in Woodstock. I had walked through a storm. I got flattened, but I was not dead.

I felt I had to do something to regain my faith, which felt like my true self, but I didn't know what that something was. Had I been let down by the greatest known healer in the world, or had I simply lacked the faith to trust in his work? I'd once said that faith wasn't an uncertainty but a tangible, potent thing that allowed me to know that what I saw was real. Bah! Humbug! I felt lonelier than I'd ever felt before. I was face to face with an arbitrary beginning that had come to a dead end. Depression slithered deeper in on me.

Creeping around the house I looked but did not see, or what I saw I wasn't sure I believed. I found myself standing, arms locked over my chest, in the front room of the bungalow. The black leather chair, the beige curtains, the computer, the gray nubby carpet were before me. There was little doubt I was observing these things as I stood there. I walked into the kitchen and recalled the mental representations of those things I'd just seen. Did the whole of what I remembered in the room come before my eyes in a simultaneous vision? As compared to the room I'd seen with my eyes—or rather one eye—the room I was remembering seemed unreal. How could I make absolutely certain that visual pictures were not things I deliberately manufactured? Were these things not directly attributable to the action of my sensory organs and nerve endings? My eyes were swimming in black.

My depression crept in harder, deeper. My thoughts were like silt, gunk, feces. I thought it was because I felt I could do something about my loss of faith, which I was beginning to call loss of self. But I didn't know what that something was. Then, I supposed, if there was such a thing as a miracle it didn't need my approval. Nature didn't need me to understand it. Maybe miracles weren't dependent on fears, hopes, reasoning, or pleading? I realized doubt killed the very idea of a miracle. My own doubt was still present. What about faith? Was it the opposite of doubt? Or did faith come from a well too deep to be measured, so mysterious and complicated that it was impossible to understand? I knew I didn't have the kind of faith needed to believe in miracles. I no longer had any faith at all.

Days wore on; at night I had fitful dreams and visions. A cliff face appeared, and I thought to jump. But the vision receded. Cowbells smacked together, and flying aliens snapped their fingers. The light beings came and put their arms around me; I was in the trench again—without the spiders. With trepidation I awaited the entities' instructions.

"We stand beside you," was all they said. Oxum lowered a cup of honey to my lips as Pai threw cowrie shells, spirals of life and death.

One night Credo Mutwa floated before me in the rushing air. He wore leopard skin and an iridescent collar made of shiny metal with rocks that dangled onto his stomach. A spear, taller than he, was poised and ready to take aim. Seeing him I felt as if I was looking through a translucent veil. He was much older than he appeared in the dream ten years ago. Back then he was a vibrant young man. Now he appeared as a grandfather. His hair was unkempt, dry, gray, and his face was wrinkled. He was an old man.

"Get up from your bed ma'am."

I was speechless. Credo Mutwa smiled, showing his evenly spaced teeth. I tried to shake myself, but it was as though I was paralyzed. My mind wandered through myriad possibilities: a visualization, a spirit, a reverie? I wanted to ignore him. I was through with spirits. But Credo was anything but easy to ignore. He seemed to be filled with blazing life force. He wouldn't disappear.

The sound of power in his voice gave me chills. "You must strike stones together," he said. "Get up! Get up! Now!"

A sudden wind kicked up in the room. Credo was holding a lantern that cast eerie shadows on the walls. He began walking into the main room. There was a pulling and throbbing motion on my body, and then I was able to move an arm and a leg. I rolled out of bed and followed him. Credo directed me to stand in the center of the room. He pointed down to a table against the wall. "Please, ma'am. Pick up those stones over there."

I couldn't find my tongue to respond, but I was able to walk to the table where two shards of crystal lay gleaming like gems.

"Yes, ma'am. Those are the ones. I want you to strike them together," Credo said.

I picked them up; they didn't weigh more than half a pound. A shard in each hand, I clanked them together.

"No. Do it like this," he said, sending pictures into my brain like images on a video clip.

I silenced my mind, took a deep breath, and began scraping the shards together. The sound was dry and raspy. Incandescent flashes flew in the darkened room. Credo looked at me with curiosity and a little more hope. I struck them together again. The crystals gleamed with faint hues of red, yellow, and hot white. I looked at Credo. "I have gems to share with you when you come to Africa," he said. The Zulu priest was pulling on me. But why, I wondered.

And then I was upset. "No. No. I don't want to go on another wild goose chase," I said. "I don't want to see these things. I'm not going through that again."

The room was dark, cold, and quiet. Credo had vanished. I put the stones back on the table and walked into the bedroom. Forget about these visitations, I thought and got back into bed. But my thoughts hummed and chirred. What could the Zulu possibly want with me anyway? Deep down the pestering in the pit of me wouldn't let go. It was like a mantra: *Go to the Zulu. Go to the Zulu.* But I wouldn't. I didn't want to go anywhere. I didn't want to experience anything. I was too depressed. I didn't have the money, or the energy.

Days later my friend Sherry, a world traveler and entrepreneur, called to tell me she was going to South Africa to work with elephants on a reserve. "I want you to come with me," she said. "I'm going to pay your way."

An acquaintance is inviting me to Africa? Is this for real? Again? This was just like the time when a friend showed up to make sure I got to Guatemala to meet Carlos. Then Josie turned up in a magazine article and got me to Brazil. Now Sherry was bringing me to South Africa. In each of these instances it seemed there was a destiny conductor who arrived at my station, rang a bell, and I got on board. There was no report from the doctors about the cancer. It was a time of "Let's wait and see."

Credo had found a way to bring me to him.

Be What You Are
Called to Be

— ∽ —

Nature shows us only the tail of the lion. But I do not doubt the lion belongs to it even though he cannot at once reveal himself because of his enormous size.

ALBERT EINSTEIN

ONE WHO CAUSES THINGS TO ASCEND

March 2004

I am driving through a wavering tunnel of lacy grasses tall as an elephant. I think of the sea of green trees I'd once flown over on my way to Manaus, heading to the casa for the first time. Though that trip seems a world away, it mirrors this trip. The light. The ultramarine sky. But here I am trying to evade desperation. Losing faith was so painful, I wonder if I will ever be happy again. I don't know how to unburden myself, but having made the choice to come here seems to be a start.

After Sherry convinced me to join her I managed to reach Credo's mobile phone and got permission to visit him. I flew from New York with a stopover in Frankfurt, planning to meet Sherry later to go on safari. A white Afrikaner woman named Jane who ran the farm at Naledi—Credo's compound in the Magaliesberg Mountains, an hour northwest of Johannesburg—met me at the airport. She was a physically fit, redheaded extrovert in her fifties who looked like she had lived much of her life in the sun.

Disoriented from two days of travel, I followed Jane from baggage claim into an elevator to a multilevel parking lot beneath the terminal.

Jane led me to a new, white van, and I sat up front with her as we drove up the ramp into the bright African sun ablaze in a blue sky. The light was concentrated and thick, like the streamline beam I created in childhood by focusing the sun with a magnifying glass to set scraps of paper on fire.

"Look at the grass!" I said. "It's so fluid and silky. Look at its tufts and tassels! It moves in waves, like flocks of birds flying in tandem."

Jane looked at me askance. "It is just grass. What are you talking about?"

After about forty-five minutes we turned onto a rutted, dusty, red dirt road full of potholes. The grasslands were swallowed up by thick brush, knotted vines, and towering trees—a green, shadowy world that contrasted with the expansive, sun-drenched flatlands along the highway. Gazing out the windows of our air-conditioned vehicle I saw women walking barefoot on the roadside, babies slung across their backs and bundles balanced on their heads. I saw unremitting poverty. We passed a huge fenced-in area, a breeding farm where ostriches strode like giant sandpipers.

Credo's compound was a little farther along, through iron gates. The grass was cut short on either side of a long dirt driveway. Jane pointed out his house: a single-story wooden building with a large front porch. We stopped in front of a brick building another couple of hundred yards farther along, which was used to house the international guests who came to see Credo. I disembarked and stretched, feeling the glorious freshness and warmth of the air. Red-billed gray ibises flew overhead, screaming *Ha-De-Da, Ha-De-Da,* the name by which they were known here. An untended meadow dipped down to a rushing stream. The thickly forested Magaliesbergs, topped with craggy rock spires, rose up beyond the stream, one hundred million years older than the Himalayas. If the Tigris and Euphrates Valley was the cradle of civilization, then this area of Africa was the cradle of *Homo sapiens.*

The place had an ancient, primeval feel. I wanted to take off my shoes and race out across the meadow toward the stream, but the gardener and his wife, Mapula—a beautiful, dark-skinned woman dressed in pale pink—advised against it.

"You can't go out in the grass, because the snakes are running," Mapula said.

That slowed me down.

She added that I was not to stand under trees, because the green mambas, poisonous snakes, dropped from them onto the heads and shoulders of the unsuspecting. She also warned me against vipers, coral snakes, and other deadly species. I saw that she carried a knobbery, a stick that she told me was used for flushing and killing snakes in the grass. I soon found a wooden branch, which I would hold before me as I toured the compound, tapping the ground with wary anticipation.

Mapula had recently returned from the hospital for treatment from a black mamba bite. The snake had struck her on the ankle as she was walking to the guesthouse to work. She showed me the V scar on the back of her Achilles tendon. "The black mamba is nearly always fatal," Mapula said. "One hundred percent. But I survived! The doctors said it was magic." She laughed.

I glanced up and happened to see Credo. His large, round form, lumbering like a bear, receded as he headed for what Mapula told me was the Healing Village. I wanted to run over and introduce myself, but I sensed he needed to be somewhere (I would later find out that this was the first time he had entered the village in months), and I didn't want to intrude.

I unpacked in the guesthouse, which Jane told me was called Naledi, the evening star. I had a small sleeping room with a patio overlooking the mountains. I flopped down on the bed and thought about Brazil. Before João operated on my eye three years ago my desire to connect with him had been tinged with sadness. I had somehow known I would discover loss. I didn't know if I would ever have the kind of faith João spoke of. Yet here I was in Africa. Was I still hoping to find faith?

That evening Jane and I sat on the back porch eating Braai, or barbeque chicken, with *melies* (corn on the cob) and green salad, listening to the rush of the stream, the buzz and trill of insects, and the ear piercing shrieks of the Ha-De-Das. As I looked at Jane my mind screamed,

I've had cancer and I'm still sore from the operations! But Jane didn't know.

At nightfall bats flitted under the porch canopy. The southern constellations were bright in a moonless sky. Frogs began croaking all around us—tasty morsels for the snakes. Jane told me stories about Credo and showed me a first edition of his book, *Indaba, My Children,* on ancient Bantu teachings and the secret knowledge known as Umlando. In the cover photo Credo was a young man, draped in a leopard skin with his spear poised, ready for battle. He looked exactly as he had in my dream ten years ago.

I woke up to a brilliant sun shining through the windows and four dogs howling outside my door. I washed, dressed, and went to the main house. Mapula, her hair pulled back in a pale pink scarf, had a massive pile of ironing in front of her. She told me she was saving bus money to go to Malawi where the AIDS epidemic raged. She felt a deep call to help the suffering. We snuck time together—Jane, her boss, scolded her when she talked to guests. I was ushered into the breakfast room where I ate paw-paw and drank coffee. Then it was time to go to Credo. Mapula pointed me toward his house.

Walking through the compound, baboons screamed in the mountains. I was amazed by the variety in the Magaliesberg landscape: dry veld bordering lush, verdant valley. A ring of large volcanic rocks naturally etched with lines and figures—called elephant stones, I would later learn—surrounded a massive oak. I glanced to my left. In an open meadow one hundred yards in the distance was the African Healing Village that Credo built, with its beehive hut, a pyramid, and a rondavel hut.

At the house an African woman answered my knock on the screen door. Her face was open and warm.

"I've come to meet Credo Mutwa," I told her. "He's expecting me."

Credo was sitting on a broad couch in the living room. "Please, please, come in," he said in a soft, lilting voice.

I moved toward him and greeted him, offering my name but not my hand; I knew that traditional shamans were never to be touched without an invitation. He was eighty-two years old, with thick spectacles, mahogany skin, and long, wild gray hair, like an artist Einstein. He had an androgynous quality. I felt as if I was talking to an archetypal grandfather and grandmother, a primal goddess and a warrior chieftain.

"Sir, what is the proper protocol for addressing you?" I asked. I felt energized, lucid, which was odd as I should have been exhausted after two days of air travel.

"You may call me Credo, honorable one. Will you please be seated, ma'am, on the couch there?"

Credo's partner Virginia—a woman of about sixty, dressed in traditional sangoma attire, a South African of Khoisan ancestry—sat down beside him. Her skirt was black with a pattern of red roosters surrounded in glowing halos. Her long hair, still black, was plaited with white and red beads that cascaded over her white top; both her wrists were circled with white bead bracelets. I could tell she was summing me up as we talked about my trip from the States. I gave simple answers, staying reserved, absorbing things in the room, and listening for clues on how to continue. I was grateful to be in Credo's presence but also at a loss as to what might come of our meeting. I'd gone through a terrible ordeal, I'd been at an all-time low. And at the same time I was very aware of the vision I'd had of the Zulu priest, and of the electric beads. I'd traveled across the world to be here.

Credo had an overwhelming presence. He was a mammoth man, round in girth, more than six feet tall, and perhaps three hundred pounds. Multiple layers of blue cotton shawls and cloths in richly colored patterns cocooned him. His bare feet, flat, without arches, pressed into the floor. A necklace of copper and stones covered his chest and hung down to his lower abdomen. This was a sacred object of power, four hundred years old, weighing more than seventy pounds, and forged by priest blacksmiths, I was told. The necklace held a human skull the size of a cantaloupe, carved from black stone. A human-size heart of green volcanic rock hung next to the skull, and below it dangled a copper breastplate in the form of a sickle moon that covered the bottom of his rib cage. Below that was a rock the size of a man's fist. Credo looked just as he had when he'd visited me in my bedroom not two months ago.

His gentle demeanor eased my discomfort in his presence, but I could not forget that he was one of the most powerful shamans in Africa. The many titles in his name—High Sanusi Vusamazulu Credo Mutwa—signified his authority. *Sanusis* were like cardinals or rinpoches, spiritual leaders and master healers. As leader of the sanusis—Credo—was known as the High Sanusi, the Chosen, the high holy man, prophet, protector of the Zulu peoples, and keeper of Zulu medical and magical knowledge. *Mutwa* meant "little Bushman," because Credo was descended, in part, from the almond-eyed people of the Kalahari who were lighter skinned than the Bantu. *Vusamazulu* meant the awakener of the Zulu, uplifter of the people, and signified "one who causes things to ascend."

He was born in KwaZulu-Natal, South Africa, on July 21, 1921. His grandfather was high priest and guardian of the tribe's history. When Credo became very ill as a child it was determined that his sickness was a call from the ancestors to become a witch doctor. Credo grew up as his grandfather's attendant, studying with him, undergoing rigorous and secret initiations, and carrying the medicine bags. In 1963 Credo Mutwa was officially proclaimed High Sanusi.

He oversaw more than five hundred traditional healers in a system that stretched back thousands of years. He presided over the sanusis, the *sangomas,* a class of mediums who communed with ancestor spirits for healing and other (mostly) beneficent purposes, and the *inyangas,* traditional African herbalists. He had been spoken of as the Father of Africa. He was an artist, architect, teacher, wisdomkeeper, storyteller, and an authority on stargazing, star beings, and the ancient art of African astrology.

The room was filling with midday light. I felt Credo's absolute authority. I was overcome with gratitude to be in his presence. I asked, with some trepidation, if I might record our conversation. Credo nodded his assent.

"Now, ma'am, why, may I inquire, are you here?" he asked.

I felt shy as I began speaking, acutely aware that I was imposing on his time. I briefly told him that I'd gone to the Amazon for healing and to Brazil to understand spirit possession. I told him about Carlos, Pai, and João. Then I described how I began to shake, jerk, and froth at the mouth when I touched his Zulu necklace, and how I'd seen him in a dream as a young man dressed in leopard skin that night.

"Since then I haven't been able to stop thinking about coming to Africa to see you," I said. "Those beads and the dream of you affected me . . . but I don't know exactly what that means."

"Yes, ma'am," he said pleasantly, nodding, as if I'd said nothing surprising.

At this point I felt myself bursting open inside. I wanted to scream out to him, "Since the dream I've had cancer and I need your help!" But I chickened out. Instead I said, "So I have come because of the necklace and the dream. I want to learn about Zulu healing. It has taken me many years to get here."

It was Credo's turn to pause. He seemed to be looking at me but beyond me, too, into a wider arena. I held my breath. When he began to speak the first few comments were general. Then he began to speak of cancer. This startled me. I had not mentioned the word. It was absolutely clear to me that he had divined my intentions.

"Most honorable one," he said addressing me with a sincerity and respect that took my breath away. "I've had cancer three times in my adult life, and I'm still alive. It was not just one kind of cancer. It was different kinds of cancer. There was a cancer that I got because I am a workman. I worked with lead fixing the gutters in housing and so on. And then lead, which was hot, fell upon my leg. After some three years, a black stuff started here on my thigh, and this black stuff was itchy and annoying, and then I went to a white-man doctor and he said, 'Hey, you've got a thing called melanoma.'

"I said, 'What is the melanoma, sir? Why is it having such a beautiful sounding name?' The doctor said, 'This thing is going to kill you. You must have your leg cut off.' I said, 'No, doctor. I am sorry, I can't. Where would you cut the leg? If you would cut the leg here, I would make myself a wooden leg and walk with that.' The doctor said, 'You must cut it right off at the top, at the hip.' I said, 'No, I'm sorry, Doctor.'

"I began to work on an enormous statue of a pregnant goddess, the Mother Goddess. I was so weak at the time my friends had to tie me to a ladder so I could finish the sculpture. I put everything into her, all my fight and joy. In my obsession to create this thing of beauty, my cancer ran away."

Now that he'd told me his story, I wanted to tell mine.

"I've just been operated on for cancer, and I am still healing," I finally confessed. "It was my second diagnosis in four years. The first time I'd had cancer, I'd been afraid. This time I'd been forewarned by spirits who told me they would protect me from the terrifying spiders I saw in a vision."

"Yes, ma'am, I understand."

"After my first diagnosis, I had nearly been destroyed by fear. But after this second time, I've lost trust. My dreams have shriveled. I don't believe in miracles. I'm not even sure why I am here," I said.

He pursed his lips together. I waited.

"Cancer is afraid of ecstasy," said High Sanusi Vusamazulu Credo Mutwa. "When the human being is in a state of excitement," he continued, "in a state of joy, then that human being becomes free of cancer because cancer doesn't like the human soul and body."

This thrilled me. It felt like he was shining bright, clear light in the face of darkness. Here was the greatest healer in Africa articulating and affirming what had been forming inside me.

"If the mind is occupied by something exhilarating, the body has a better chance to heal. Power of mind can conquer the unseen serpent, the black smoke in the heart," Credo said.

"Cancer is a hungry animal," he went on. "It feeds on fear. If there is nothing to feed on, the cancer will run away. It is not the unseen serpent that kills the person but the mind that surrenders to it."

And then he said it again: Cancer is afraid of ecstasy.

I sat in silence as the words rang in my ears. My tongue itched, and I rolled it along the roof of my mouth. Even the flies seemed suspended.

"Does ecstasy cure all forms of disease?" I finally asked.

"Do you know what ecstasy is, ma'am?"

I was shy about answering such an enormous question, but I decided to try.

"I have found that ecstasy is intense, emotional excitement. A state of exultation. An intense bliss. A communion with joy. A rushing in of inspiration. A connection to creation." I thought about the joy I'd felt during Pai's ceremonies.

"Thank you, honorable one," Credo said. "That was a valuable description of ecstasy. Would you please come tomorrow morning to my home?"

"Yes," I said, as I rose from the couch. "I'll fix the time with Virginia. Thank you very, very much."

ANCESTORS AND MEDIUMS

Credo was sitting at a table, working on a large comic book in the living room. His paints and markers were on a side table. Behind him were rows of books and an elongated tan mask with raffia-like hair and white opaque eyes seemingly lit from inside. Credo wore several fabrics wrapped about him. The undercloth was gray with Navajo-like geometric designs and was covered by a red and gold fabric patterned with what looked like magnified honeycombs. A broad, turquoise cloth with a white stripe along the edge was placed over these two fabrics.

Virginia sat beside Credo, giving him sly glances. She got up to answer the mobile, then spoke to him in Zulu. A fan made white-noise whooshing sounds. In one corner of the room there was a three-foot-high pile of black rocks. A low table held funny-looking jars, a metal spitting cobra, feathers, bark cylinders, a black pot on a long spindly tripod, and green stones the size of avocados. Above this table of objects was a surreal, seven-foot oil painting of Credo's depicting fire and volcanoes, a crimson horizon, a fighter plane, a moon, a flying television, an open newspaper, and a cigarette floating in the sky.

"What is the story of your painting?" I asked.

"It is the prediction of one of our greatest prophets," Credo said. "This man foretold the coming of a time when people would fly through the sky in eagles made of iron. These eagles would lay eggs of death onto great villages and cities to destroy them. He further said people would travel through the world in dragons made of iron and wood and that great African kings would sell their people into slavery for water that could be ignited and set alight. He further said that people would so pollute the seas that the seas would turn red with the blood of dead fishes. He went on to predict his own passing and that he would be killed by a white man with an iron pipe."

"When did he make these predictions?"

"He made this prophecy, ma'am, close to two hundred years ago, before the white people came to his land in southern Africa."

I was about to tell him what an extraordinary painting I thought it was when Credo, with a swift gesture of his chin, motioned for me to look down at the comic book. He was coloring in a very large woman.

"The comic book is painting itself more than I am painting it," he said. He showed me several finished pages. A massive woman was in every scene, exquisitely drawn. I thought the figure Amazonian, as trees, huts, and other Africans appeared small alongside her. I asked who she was.

"She is Amarava, ma'am," he said, becoming animated when saying her name. "The great inspiration of my life. This thirty-foot goddess has mighty powers of enlightenment. She is an ancestor, the Great Mother of the First People. Amarava has been my guide throughout my life. She had once commanded me to deliver the Great Knowledge, and this I did in my book *Indaba*." He'd painted her hair green, her skin red.

"You've seen her? How does she come to you?" I asked.

"She comes to me as a spirit, although she is quite real. She can come to me in physical form, which in the past made my late wife, Cecilia, weep at seeing her in our bed. She can make herself into a half-human, half-animal being. She can come in vengeance with the claws of a lion. She comes to me in dreams."

I waited, hoping he would continue. Then I primed him with the word, "Dreams? How do the dreams tell you things?"

"They are communications from the ancestors and may therefore not be ignored. Every effort must be made to understand the messages these dreams convey," he said.

"I dreamed of you, twice. Or one time, I suppose, was a visitation," I said. "You were inspirational to me, and I believe you helped bring me here."

"I was directed by such dreams to travel throughout Africa to study with my teachers. This is how an initiate is sent on the path," Credo said.

"Are there other ways the ancestors communicate with us?"

"Yes, by throwing the bones [divination] and by possessing us so that the ancestor can speak," he said. Ah, just like Umbanda, I thought. I was anxious to talk about possession and hoped I would not offend the great sanusi by bringing up the subject.

"Baba, I have been possessed by African spirits, and I would like to understand this." I found it comfortable to address him this way—Baba, Father.

"Was it more than the one time, ma'am?"

"Yes, several times. It was very, very intense. I shook. I danced. I strutted. Sometimes a spirit would speak through my mouth."

"When I was a young child Amarava possessed me. People thought it was a kind of sickness, that I was crazy. I was afraid, because I didn't know what was happening," he said. "Possession when it first happens is a profoundly disturbing experience."

I recalled the time I'd been possessed by the force in the necklace. I agreed it was excruciatingly disturbing.

"And now? Possession by the ancestors, what is it like?" I asked.

"I may not speak of this much, except to tell you the ancestor inhabits the body and communicates directly through the mouth of the person.

"Virginia, can you tell our friend what sound Ungonga, a sangoma friend of Credo's who was a practitioner of traditional Zulu medicine, made when she was healing me, with you, from the stroke?" (I'd learned from Credo that he had a stroke a few months earlier and hadn't been expected to live.) Virginia clacked her teeth together in a rhythmic umclick-click fashion. The sound churned, seeming to fold in on itself, though it was highly percussive, sizzling really.

"Listen to her, that clicking sound, the word that a sangoma makes when she acupunctures you to return feeling to a paralyzed thing," Credo said. He made the sound. "The sound," he made it again, "is *God. God. God. God. God.* It is said that human beings, before they were given a language, used to communicate with funny sounds, and they also used to communicate with the mind."

Credo and Virginia taught me clicks and whispers, buzzing zzzzzzzzzz's and ululations for healing a person. I'd heard the sounds before. I'd made them myself when spirits came inside me.

"And so, this is how it is," Credo said. He sat before me, his eyes shining. Virginia had a Cheshire cat look about her.

"Baba, may I trouble you to look at a few pictures from Brazil?" I asked. He assented.

"Here is Pai Lazaro. *Pai* means 'Baba' in Brazil."

"Yes. He's a medicine man?" He passed photos on to Virginia.

"Yes. He's a priest, and his family is from Mozambique. During ceremonies, which I have attended, he calls the African ancestors, the Orixás," I said, showing him more pictures. "Here you see his altar for Iemanjá."

He glanced at the next photo in the pile. This one was taken up close. "Goddess of the sea. She is Yemanja, which means Mother of the Waves," he said.

"Iemanjá is very important to the Brazilian people," I said.

Credo thumbed through pictures. "Is it like Voodoo?" he asked.

"Pai and his followers assimilate Christian saints with African gods during ceremony. The gods enter some of the worshippers' bodies; they have come inside me too. Yes. I guess it's like Voodoo.

"I told Pai Lazaro about you." (I'd been in e-mail communication with Ana, and she'd ferried messages to Pai.)

"He knows about me?" Credo giggled.

"He does now." I said. "He wants to visit you."

"It will be a great honor if he comes. I pray to God that I'm still alive then, because there are bad people in this place where we are who don't allow me to practice fully the sacred thing of our people. Our great ones need to be honored in ritual," he said.

"I asked Pai, if you don't give offerings to the spirits and you discontinue ceremonies for the Orixás, what would happen. He said the gods would go somewhere else, where the people would appreciate them."

"Yes. Yes. This is the thing; the gods must never, ever, ever be forgotten, ma'am. In keeping them alive, in keeping them remembered, we also gain power through them. Africans turn to their ancestors because the direct presence of the Divine is more than a human being can bear," Credo said.

"So it's important to continue?"

"Yes. These Orixás are what we call the great ancestors, the ones who came before us, who came with much suffering, much, much torture. They came before us and showed us the way."

"They were alive at one point? Ogum was a human being before he became a god? Or was he always a god?" I asked.

"He was always a god, ma'am. From other worlds he came. Some gods were once people who have been deified over the centuries. Some gods were beings from other worlds who came to this Earth to, how do you say, to pave the way."

"I think the ancestors have been forgotten in America," I said. "Or, I wasn't taught about those who came before me. I don't know where I came from. I don't know about my family past, or how it affects me."

"Those who fear the knowledge of the old ones who have come before have deliberately broken it. It may be broken, but it will one day come back to the surface," he said. "Thus, human beings will run away briefly from god and the spirit, but they never really escape." He let out a belly laugh. "Never. It's like a man driving along the road and convincing himself that there are no traffic cops, until one of them stops him and gives him a ticket."

"There aren't many people in the world getting tickets these days," I said.

Credo guffawed. "All the traffic cops are sleeping a little bit."

Perhaps a minute passed, and the tenor of our conversation changed. I felt Credo looking both at me and through me, patiently waiting for me to speak. I looked down at the floor.

"Yes?" I asked softly.

"I feel that you have traveled a long way."

"Yes, most honorable one," I replied. "It has taken me ten years to get here. I had to go to the Amazon jungle, to central Brazil, to many priests, healers, and wise people before I could come to you."

"Ma'am, may I respectfully say that the journey is much longer than that? Please tell me the names of your grandfathers."

"I think my forebears came from England, Scotland, Ireland, and Holland. I know only one name," I said. I told him one of the family names—Rugnion—and he was intrigued.

"That is very unusual," he said. "I think it is French."

"Maybe."

"No, ma'am. Not maybe. It is not Celtic. It is not German."

"No."

"It is not Israelite. It is definitely Norman French, descendants from Norse Viking conquerors."

"These are things that I never think about."

"You should pay close attention to your people, ma'am. Our ancestors explain much about our lives, who we are, and why we do what we do."

Even when you feel the ancestors don't belong to you? I wondered.

"Ancient people like Eric the Red and many others visited the Americas," he said. "They, together with Africans and Phoenicians, were the true discoverers of America."

"Yes. I believe that's true."

"It is not surprising that you are descended from these people. Without knowing it, you are following in the footsteps of people long, long ago."

"I don't quite follow. What do you mean?"

"It is important, ma'am, to understand what your ancestors were doing. Why did they venture into the unknown? Why did they take the risk? Can you imagine what it was like to sail across the Atlantic in the little boats they had? How many of them perished, how difficult the journey must have been? Can you imagine how afraid they were? They must have been viewed as brave, but more than a little bit crazy. Why did they go to such lengths? What were they looking for?"

"I think of Odysseus, Baba," I said. "He went to Troy for war but found on his long journey home that something was missing in his soul."

THE HEALING HUT

Brandishing the knobbery Mapula had given me I walked on the footpath through tall grass to the healing hut at the center of Credo's village. I was wearing a pale blue shirt, my legs were covered in khakis, and I wore boots to protect myself from the dangerous snakes I'd seen on previous walks. The fragrant smell of eucalyptus hung in the air. The weather was changeable—the air hot, ionized. I stood for a moment on the red dirt path furrowed out by flash floods. The ground striations looked like ancient, primeval rock art. Butterflies swarmed in trees with thirty-foot-high twisted trunks. The village was surrounded by a hand-hewn fence of thick branches that poked from the ground in wild twists and turns. In traditional villages this type of barrier was built to keep out lions and other predators.

Inside the fence Credo had built and decorated a pyramid. The roof was covered in short, gray-colored grass that was as thick and impenetrable looking as AstroTurf. Next to it was a pumpkin-colored concrete beehive with a conical roof and large, white eyes painted over a turquoise mouth. The mouth was the door. There was a third hut, a round ceremonial structure with astrological symbols, animals, and eyes—African hieroglyphics—painted in a ring beneath its conical thatched roof. I walked over to the healing hut. I'd been with Credo several days, and he'd asked me to come to the village. This, I'd learned from Mapula, was a great honor.

I peeked in and there was Credo.

"Please, please, come in," he said.

Beams of light flooded the entranceway, but the interior was dark and still. Inside was a central peristyle. Colorful African astrological signs and symbols, painted by Credo, revolved around the ceiling: a large eye, stars, an intertwined pair of snakes, a dolphin floating under the thatched roof.

Credo's thick hands rested on his stomach; his bare feet were firmly planted on the pounded dirt floor. Virginia, in her sangoma attire, sat across from him, also barefoot. Her eyes were soft.

"Please, honorable one, would you sit next to Virginia?"

I nodded wordlessly.

The High Sanusi was draped in several wraps. He wore a thick copper necklace etched with dolphins, ciphers, symbols, and spaceships. The markings on the surface were artistic like an etching on a printing plate. Suspended from hand-hewn chains were sculpted male and female figures, each seven inches in length. The female, carved of dark stone, had voluptuous breasts and hips. The male figure was pale green, had large, slanting oval eyes, a round head, an opening for its nose, and a slit for a mouth. An alien, I thought. There were oddly shaped rocks dangling from the breastplate part of the necklace, which originally belonged to an ancient chief named Mpepu. A human-size outstretched woman's hand of beaten copper inscribed with constellations and symbols hung down the center of the necklace. On her three middle fingers an elaborate medallion hung. (I would later learn from Credo that this was the Necklace of Mysteries, which was more than four hundred years old.)

A long, breathless silence settled between the three of us. The High Sanusi closed his eyes, sat quietly for several minutes, then let out a shallow breath. When he was ready, he stood clasping a dark oval object. Virginia rose and went to him. She lit a match. A small flame flicked unsteadily then quickly cast a thin veil of shimmering light across the hut.

Credo's gaze was downcast as he spoke, "Now, ma'am, a terrible war was fought in Natal between the British and the Zulu. When Zulu men refused to work for the British they were massacred by machine guns and hung from trees in gruesome display." He paused, looking into the distance. "The Zulu women devised a plan to hide their husbands and sons from the English colonists. Dressing the men in women's clothing, they placed them in the fields to work. When the British arrived, they saw only women.

"The Zulu women stopped the last great war in Natal," he said. "When the war ended they melted their bracelets and ornaments and made the Lamp of Peace."

Credo lifted the lamp.

"Whenever we think and we remember these brave Zulu women we light this lamp so that as it shines, peace will come to us everywhere in the world, not only in Africa but to all lands," he said.

Credo Mutwa paused.

"Oh God, you who are everywhere. You who brought us to this world, here to serve our stay until we have purified ourselves of all anger, bitterness, revenge, and greed, we ask you, oh God: Let the Lamp of Peace shine, and when at the end of time the weary universe grinds toward its ending and the darkness recalls each fugitive star, each fugitive world, let the Lamp of Peace be the one thing remaining in that eternal void, until the voice of God is heard again and creation is reborn."

I was surprised that his prayer sounded Christian. I'd read in a book that his mother had raised him as a Christian the first years of his life. He seemed to be synthesizing as I wanted to do, so I understood his combining ancient Zulu with modern Christianity. I wanted to understand my Christian upbringing in relation to my desires and needs to practice aboriginal, ancient religion. When I said "God. God. God," I sometimes thought of Jesus Christ too. When he spoke in Zulu, I got the sense his high god was different from the God he spoke to in English. And yet Zulu religion included a belief in a creator god, Nkulunkulu, the aged, the first, the most revered one.

The High Sanusi set the lamp carefully on his stool, exchanging it for a heavy, welded sword. Virginia bent down to retrieve a four-foot ankh made of shiny metal. On the hilt and blade of each were carved astrological symbols. The sanusi and sangoma sang softly, possibly in Zulu. The song was soft, winsome, mellifluous. They began circling one another, the weighty swords held with both hands at arms length. The spectacle of the great sanusi and his sangoma in mock battle was mesmerizing. Each one attacked the other, parried and evaded blows. The metal rang and clanked. Credo and Virginia rushed together as if for the final blow. Deftly they looped their arms, pressing their bodies together. Instead of breaking away to attack again, the handheld weapons were ritually exchanged. Virginia was holding the sword as the High Sanusi clutched the ankh.

"It is said there will come a time when the man shall take his weapon of killing and hand it over to the woman, then and only then, in the closing years of Earth's existence as we know it, shall there be peace on Earth," Credo solemnly proclaimed.

Credo requested I return to the healing hut in two hours.

I had my tape recorder in hand, ready to turn it on as I always did when meeting with Credo. He was waiting for me on the far side of the temple in a black cloth robe, wearing a huge copper necklace with hand-worked chains that held a sun, a moon, an etched disc, raw stones, a smooth, largish green oval disc, a scimitar-shaped lower breastplate, and a seven-inch ankh that dangled onto his belly.

It was relatively cool inside the hut. The walls, made of stone, were thick, and there were no windows. Virginia sat on the bench across from Credo. Next to her was Ayize, a Zulu woman in her early fifties. I was told to sit with Virginia and Ayize—across from Credo. Ayize's name meant, "Let it happen." I'd come to understand that African names given at birth were meant to assist the human being in understanding the key principles of life.

The hut seemed to be filled with overwhelming soundlessness. I focused intently on the High Sanusi. I had no idea what was coming. He began a lecture, speaking with style, cogency, and grace.

"To us Africans the skull is the holiest part of the human bone system," he said. "The human skull—or the house of the soul—is a sacred space where the self resides as a tiny, shining star, a star filled with great knowledge that can be accessed. Our people, my people, the Zulus, call a skull *ukakayi*. The word means 'the immortal one,' the one who goes on and on and on."

Credo's impeccable English was delivered in a soft, lilting voice with lubricated vowels and rolled Rs.

"The neck is the dwelling place of beauty," he went on. "From the neck area come the beautiful sounds when a human being sings. It is there where the song of communication resides. Lower still is the heart soul, controlling the lungs, heart, and spleen. Zulus know the area below this is the nourisher soul. Women have a fourth soul, which we call the gateway. This is the soul that rules the coming of children. Women can also produce a nonphysical child who is born but never seen by others. These children are recognized by African people just as physical children and are given names and honored.

"Is there a question on that?" he asked.

"Please, sir, is a nonphysical child like a vision or a dream?" I asked.

"This is what white people call a phantom pregnancy. Because we believe that in this creation," Credo stated, "in this universe, nothing is unreal. All is real. All is there. If you dream a dream, that dream does not just go away. It becomes there, so you must treat it as if it was real. There are many laws that govern our behavior and our reaction to our dreams. And this roughly is what our people believe."

He touched the fabric of his clothes and continued, "We do not make the distinction in Africa between the visible and invisible—what Westerners consider the imagined and the real. One must act accordingly, for nothing is unreal."

"Baba, how do dreams tell us about the future?" I asked softly.

"Dreams are living reality," the High Sanusi said. "*Enas* send important messages through dreams. Ma'am, when a child is born it does not possess a self. This self, or ena, develops at birth, and as the child grows and is formed and nourished the ena grows. The ena is the self, shaped like the person but made from spirit substance. In the great ocean called Time, those things that are spirit, such as souls and enas, are a little bit ahead of our physical bodies. They can bring back messages or knowledge of what might happen in the future via dreams. The ena can bring warning of disease or disaster, and, if the person is listening to this warning, the disaster might be avoided."

"And if I have a dream in which a fearful message has been sent, what should I do?" I asked.

"You must act on the dream, ma'am. And you must give fear no place inside you, otherwise, it will eat you."

The High Sanusi continued his lecture, describing a snake-like entity who lived at the base of the spine and linked each of us to the unseen world. As I listened to his words a strange sensation came over me. He pronounced a magical word—or something like a word—and my body trembled. He intoned the Bushmen's name for the sacred snake, and a shudder ran through me. Ncumu. The word was a mix of clicking sounds, then something smooth, ending with a smacking of the lips like a kiss. This word, this invocation, this kiss, was unearthly and divine. When the High Sanusi sounded it again I vibrated like a quivering sheet of lightning. Everything was in roaring motion. Space blurred. It existed, and yet it did not. I was present, and yet I was not.

Then I began to drift; my consciousness slipped and shifted, though I could still hear Credo's voice. "Now this Ncumu is a creature like a snake, but a very thin, tiny snake, which is about a yard long. It is situated in the pelvis, in the lower coccyx area. It is born with you, and like your soul, it is immortal."

The High Sanusi smacked and clicked the word again and again. Ncumu. The force inside me shot higher and higher, just like when I'd touched the sangoma necklace long, long ago. Somehow I was looking through Credo's eyes into the invisible world. But a sentence formed that I understood on a level that's difficult enough to understand much less explain: *These are not his eyes, and they are not mine.* My spirit was in the nonphysical world, and, though my ears listened and my eyes watched, I knew that my soul was communing with a powerful, mysterious force, something utterly divine.

Ayize was still sitting next to me. I realized for the first time since meeting her that she was very ill. Without understanding what I was doing I touched her shoulder. I embraced her and slowly lowered her onto the bench we were sitting on. I could see sickness in her, and the sickness was speaking. Not words, but it was speaking.

I got her to lie on her stomach. I was not behaving like myself, and then I heard sounds reverberating in my body, spontaneously and without thought—humming, gurgling, moaning, growling—as I touched her in different places. I was engulfed, possessed. My diaphragm filled, lifting my torso. My tongue curled and uncurled just outside open lips. The few and fairly sparse thoughts that were forming leaped around in fragments.

When my hands found a certain spot above her shoulder blade I began pulling on it compulsively without physically touching her. With my face some inches above this point on her back, I started sucking and spitting foulness onto the floor. I coughed with choking sensations. Animal-like sounds erupted from me. I bit the air above Ayize, chomping with loud clicking noises. I was sucking out the sickness then ripping it apart with my teeth and spitting it out. My chest thumped ferociously.

Credo continued speaking as I worked on her. "This Ncumu can be activated when you are healing a person," he said. "You will feel the Ncumu rising like hot water being poured out of a kettle. It rises from the bottom of your spine. It goes along your spinal column right up through the hole under the skull, and it bursts out through the top of your skull. And then it goes on and on and on."

His voice was so distant I couldn't really follow it, but fortunately my tape recorder was rolling. "Where does that energy go?" The High

Sanusi asked. "It goes up with your Ncumu to the land of eternal life. When you are there you see all those of your friends who have got sickness on them, all the people who have got pain, you see them. And then you have the urge to touch them, and so to heal them. This is how it is."

Whatever I had been doing to Ayize was finished, and I returned to my body. Ayize smiled at me. We both sat up and glanced at Virginia, who sat quietly listening to Credo. He made no outward acknowledgment of the healing that had taken place. He talked about reincarnation for about twenty minutes then stopped to ask if I would return to the healing hut after dinner. Virginia said, "No. Baba, you need rest."

We made plans to meet the next morning after breakfast.

ECSTASY IS NCUMU

That night there was no moon, the stars were bright, and the sky shone as a dark light. Deep, explosive, double-noted hoots of an eagle owl sounded. Then suddenly all the night animals, all sounds, stopped. Maybe it was my imagination but even the wind cut out. I paused for a moment noticing my body felt different. I could feel every muscle, every bone. The muscles were smooth, elongated, relaxed. My head was in a whirl, a light pleasant trance. Tears were rolling down my cheeks. I was back at Naledi in the room Jane had assigned me.

Today I had the revelation of revelations! I was overcome with gratitude for Credo. He had begun my training by telling me cancer is afraid of ecstasy. Ecstasy was Ncumu. And now, beyond my wildest imaginings, Ncumu had descended into me in full glory. I hadn't really fully understood what possession could do until Credo showed me in the healing hut. Ncumu was God coursing through me, a force that had a life of its own. Ecstasy healed Ayize, and it healed me in ways that had been wounded even beyond the cancer.

I wondered at the differences and similarities of the healings in Africa and those I'd participated in in Ecuador. During a ceremony with Carlos I had experienced a full-blown possession. An Amerindian warrior spirit entered me. The entity had purpose and what seemed a supernatural force that turned my body into a conduit for his healing powers. I had been surprised and shocked at the unexpectedness of being possessed. It was strong, and somewhat like what I felt in Credo's presence. Both had been ecstatic possessions. Perhaps my further training had allowed a more potent form of the power to enter me in the healing hut? I wasn't sure. But I knew that the power in each instance came from Source. The purpose of both possessions was healing. The possessions were different *only* because they took place in unique and distinctive rituals. One Zulu. One Shuar. And because of the form of energy these possessions had taken in me—one as a spirit, medicine man; the other as Ncumu, pure Force.

I was thrilled knowing that something I'd struggled to understand for so long was becoming clearer. I'd wanted to allow spirit to inhabit me. I'd wanted to help others. Although my work as a medium with João expanded my awareness of the invisible world and helped me to connect with spirit healers, my newly acquired abilities had reached another apex with Credo.

I'd had cancer twice. I'd searched for faith, for ecstasy, and embodied the power that heals. I felt whole for the first time, in my life. All these years my body had been preparing to take it in. It had gotten stronger with Carlos, João, and Pai. This time, though, in the healing hut I was not considering my control or lack of control as I had during Pai's ceremonies. I was not worried about me, only that I get out of the way so Ncumu could do its work. I still didn't really know what Ncumu was. But I knew I would align myself with it, honing my body to accept more and more.

Ecstasy was the creative act. It must be everywhere, come from everywhere, I thought. It was in the air, in our mouths, in the sea, in the heavens, in space, in the mind, outside the mind. It was life itself.

In the past I'd always wondered if I was spiritual enough. But I realized everything has a spiritual side. Everything was made of spirit. Rocks and people and animals and trees had spirit in them. Spirit was everywhere. I, too, was a spirit. You can't get more spiritual than that, I thought. Yet again, I decided to make a list.

1. The force of Ncumu is real, and a direct experience of holiness. It is the oldest source, the life force. God. Ecstasy. Even the Orixás and the entities—different aspects of the Godhead—are made of Ncumu. The power in the beads was Ncumu. The healing force I felt during my apprenticeship with Carlos was Ncumu. I believe the universal force could splinter into being Iansã, Iemanjá, Exú, Dr. Cruz, Dr. Augusto. It could splinter into Shuar spirits. It could splinter into angels. But there is no personification with Ncumu. Ncumu is the undifferentiated force, before the Orixás, before the entities.

2. This is why I came to Africa, why I had to come. I had to be possessed by Ncumu. Mutwa, Credo's other name that meant the little Bushman, had given me the oldest, purest form of healing there is.

3. I now know awareness comes from direct experience with Ncumu. It is awareness and action that moved me beyond belief to faith. I can't prove Ncumu to anyone else. People have to find proof of God and faith for themselves. No one else can clear anyone else's doubt. Until you experience something, it is not real for you.

Credo's mother had given him a Latin name. *Credo* means "I trust," or "I believe." When the infinitive *credere* ends with an *o*, the verb is in first person singular. *Credo* doesn't mean she, or he, or they believe. It means "I believe."

At last I felt at peace with my childhood Christianity. I'd felt wholeness back then, long ago, in the shaking tent. I hadn't felt it for years, not since my childhood, but then, I still remembered it. That indelible, higher power was in me, and I knew it.

Having faith and trusting was a gift I'd fought for, fought against. I'd taken my time suffering as a skeptic, always resisting. No more was I letting my mind question faith and possession. My mind was not churning with confusion, not bickering with circular questions. Faith by definition was the act of stopping the questions. I had the proof I required, and I had faith in God. Nothing was wrong, and everything felt right. Doubt had been the biggest obstacle in my life.

The next morning Credo said to me, "You will heal Ayize."

The words formed themselves in front of my mind's eye as though they were written out. The most powerful shaman in Africa, perhaps in the world, had just said to me, "You will heal Ayize." Not, "You may try to heal Ayize," but "You *will* heal Ayize." It was at once an invitation and a prediction. I wondered at Credo's faith in me. I did not waste time or energy on questioning myself. I accepted this and would go to her. Virginia would be with me.

Ennis, a six-year-old boy who lived with Credo and Virginia, took me to another building in the compound. We entered a small cottage; the entryway doubled as a kitchen and living area. On one side were a gray Formica table, chairs, and two cupboards above. Beyond a stuffed chair was a door to a bedroom. We knocked and walked inside. The room was slightly dim with thick walls painted a cool light blue. Beneath a small window sat the bed, high off the floor. Ayize was lying there, half covered with a thin, dainty-flowered sheet, unpressed but clean. She lay on her stomach. There was a small, wooden chair in the middle of the room and a stool by the bed. I took off my shoes and sat on the stool. For a few moments we were quiet. Ayize glanced at me sideways then shut her eyes.

Virginia came along the bedside. We looked at Ayize's back, at the place where I felt compelled to focus yesterday. There, a huge welt had risen, like a boil: a mound crisscrossed with dozens of tiny scars. This was *not* on her back the previous day. Her skin had been smooth and clear. When I sucked at her I'd placed my mouth above her body; my hands had gently touched and circled the area. I could not have physically caused this horrible lump on her back.

I slowly moved my hand forward a little and back along her back. I tried to sense this thing but got little from my hand.

"Does it hurt?" I asked.

She shrugged, but I couldn't tell if her gesture was a yes or a no. I touched her back lightly, which brought a response. "I can move my shoulder some," she said softly.

I shook my head and wondered if I was qualified to help her. I hadn't done this before. Seeing her in front of me now was vastly different from being consumed by the healing force. I looked over to Virginia, who watched wordlessly. I sat, listening to the rustling on the tin roof, deciding what to do.

"Last night I had a dream," Ayize said in an almost imperceptible voice. "A large animal was pawing on my back, and this morning there are scratches there."

"Well the marks are on your back. That is true," I said.

I wanted the Ncumu to return to me; I believed it could heal her. I couldn't. But nothing came. Sound didn't erupt from my belly. There were no laboring animal moans or spirit talk. Only the rustling sounds above could be heard, only Virginia's quiet breathing. I inhaled deeply, hoping some illumination would come to my mind, which was frighteningly empty. I didn't know what to do. How lame I seemed to be. At least I realized that Ayize needed to feel safe.

I willed my consciousness to shift, asked for help, and began to work on her deliberately, using two small black stones—one grooved and polished from the Amazon basin, the other of volcanic rock I'd collected in my travels and always carried with me. This way of healing will have to do, I thought. That idea annoyed me. Thinking and healing didn't work well together. I had to push back thoughts to continue. I pulled out the polished stone from the jungles of Ecuador—finely smoothed by a craftsman, perhaps centuries ago—and focused it at the dark spot on Ayize's back. Immediately I felt something—a force—releasing from her. The force took the form of black smoke and rose to my eye level, hanging in the air. Ayize was silent, lying very still.

I reached back into my bag for singing crystals Credo had requested I purchase at a shop in a bordering town the week before. I rubbed two of the small ones together and—yes!—electricity flashed and a high-pitched sound rang out. Suddenly Ayize moaned, her back tensed, arching dramatically; then, just as quickly, she relaxed. The black smoke dispersed into tiny flecks that dissolved before my eyes. I moved my hands over her, and when I came to a particular place I felt two sharp pains in my own lower back. I placed Brazilian quartzes over those places on Ayize's back, and the pain in mine subsided. These stones and crystals focused healing force, but they were not the healing energy. I finished by massaging her body all the way down to her feet, feeling for areas that needed attention. A vibrant energy was moving through her. A beautiful, pale pink light emanated from her left side and a pale blue one from her right side. She fell into a deep, quiet sleep.

SPIRIT TALK AND
LION'S SONG

The day after I worked on Ayize we were sitting in Credo's living room.

"Now, ma'am," he said to me, "are you a healer?"

"No," I said, "I am not."

"No?"

To my embarrassment, Credo and Virginia laughed, almost mocking me, and making me feel very foolish as I sat there. There was something startlingly normal about his statement. Yet at the same time it made me apprehensive. Would I ever call myself a healer? I would not. The power that came from Ncumu, God, was what healed

Credo wrapped his shawl tighter, his head bent down toward his left shoulder. Softly he began: "Among the things that I am keeper of there are many things. Over there, hidden in very plain sight, is that green head. That is the oldest artifact that we keep. It was carved thousands of years ago at a time when our people still lived in caves."

I gasped at the beauty of the green, life-size head.

"This is the Great Earth Mother. Rather a fitting lady, I think. Now, on one cheek you'll see the symbol of the sun, on the other cheek the symbol of the moon, and at the back of her head you'll see a diagram showing the Sirius star system. Stories say that this head was part of a large statue that was assembled in pieces with clay and sand like a building, and only this part is left.

"It's very powerful," I said, admiring and touching the statue's head. Goosebumps rose on my arms.

"Yes, considering that it was made by human beings who used only stone tools. The first God worshipped by our people was God the Mother. While people worshipped the Mother God there was no war on Earth. People had no language then; they just made funny sounds. It is said that one day out of the sky came strange creatures, which we call the Chedongwoolie. They put disorder on Earth by giving human beings language. Human beings used to communicate with funny sounds. They also used to communicate with the mind. But today we speak, and we think we are clever. But language brought disunity. Language brought weakness to us. You often hear some religious people making funny sounds. These people who are talking in tongues are actually talking exactly as our great ancestors used to talk."

"Um hum," Virginia said, "the language of our ancestors." Sounds came from Virginia that made the room feel soft, wooly. It was as if the spirit talk was putting me to sleep, or rather putting me into an altered state of consciousness.

"When a sangoma makes the sounds that she makes, she is actually talking. People who talk that way become more ritually powerful than people who talk like we do. There are things, which we can't express in words, that we can express in thought. Why, ma'am, is not this healing being brought back?"

"I think most people are afraid because the sounds seem intense and frightening to them," I said.

"And repression, ma'am." Credo said. "The Christian churches and Islamic religion will not allow a return to that, because it is part of the Great Knowledge, the mother knowledge, by which our people lived and died."

Credo and Virginia began muttering strange and raucous sounds, teaching me how to do it. I was to use a certain sound when I knew people were in acute physical discomfort. "Because this word is very powerful in driving pain away," Credo said. I was also given sounds for driving feisty ghosts away and others that cured certain sicknesses. It is not possible for me to translate these sounds into words.

"I know these sounds," I said. I explained that spirit talk was familiar to me, because they were sounds I made in trance.

"Yes. These are very healing sounds. But you must make them with a number of people at your side."

Credo made a sound like ululating. "That again is *God. God. God.* The ancient people spoke this way."

"Are there questions you want to ask please? The law says I am not allowed to tell people anything unless they wish to know," Credo said, even though he had just taught me healing sounds without my asking.

He wanted to pass another chunk of knowledge on to me, I realized, but I had to ask the right question. Because he had explained spirit sounds and healing, I decided to ask him about healing touch.

"Now, among our healers we have got a way of healing a person, if you touch them gently. You hook your right index finger in the right index finger of the sick person, and by so doing you will feel the power flowing through you. Gently like, like . . . I don't know like what. You will feel this power flowing into this person. And you will also feel something from this person flowing to you. It is not simply a one way traffic thing. It is a two-way, or three-way, or four-way traffic thing."

Virginia answered the mobile. We sat quietly for a moment as she spoke in Zulu. When she was finished, Credo went on.

"When you are healing you must not merely feel the person's energy. You must depict it in your mind. Human beings have the power to depict things and so bestow on them something or remove that something. So, if you feel this person has got a something in him, you must ask 'What is that something?' 'What does your mind tell you that something's like?'

"One way is to depict the thing as a stone, a round stone spinning in emptiness. When you see it you can reach out with your spiritual hand, take out that stone, and throw it out."

Credo moved his hand as if he were extending it into an invisible whirlpool. He grabbed something I couldn't see and shook it away from his body.

"What you are talking about is not visualization, where one creates an image in the brain," I said. "The images generate from *their* will and place themselves in view. Are these depictions found in a place of manifestation before they are in physical reality?"

"Yes, ma'am. You must increase your awareness and learn to pay attention to the unseen. Listen and feel at a different level," Credo said.

"Among our people we use the so-called flywhisk. Or, you can use a little broom made of soft flexible grass. You just sweep this thing away from the person and throw it out.

"Always, depiction is important in African healing. But not all illness should be thrown out of the person. You must be able to know which illness should be encouraged to stay in the person and which illness should be taken and thrown outside of the person. There are sicknesses, ma'am, that are beneficial to the human being. There are sicknesses that are not beneficial to the human being. For example, all sangomas have reached a certain stage of development and are always attached by something that looks like a sickness. So you must be able to distinguish what is what.

"But you must be careful," Credo cautioned. "Healers who are good, they give out so much love to the sick people that they cause themselves to have diabetes. Contrary to what some people say, diabetes is not a disease that is caused by people leading a very funny lifestyle, eating too much and so on. It is a disease caused by giving, giving life to others, and holding people's hands.

"Then there are people who, when they are sick, or even not sick, become vampires. When you heal such people, after they go, you find yourself so weak you are like a bicycle tube that goes 'chungk, chungk, chungk.' You feel like the dogs dinner. Always, a healer must, after healing people, make himself a nice bath of salt water and sit in it allowing the steam to reach you, and thus, regain your energy."

I thanked Credo for these important teachings, noting that I would remember and use what he had taught me. "As you know, I am traveling the next two weeks. But I'll be back to see you and Virginia," I said. "Frankly, I wish I didn't have to leave. I am learning so much from you."

"Where will you go?" Credo asked. I told him I would be visiting the Kruger Game Park and Timbavati Game Reserve in Mpumalanga, in the northeastern part of South Africa and Limpopo National Park on the border of Mozambique.

"First you must go and see the footprint of the Heavenly Princess," Credo said. According to his book on Umlando—and held sacred by the ancient African tribes people of Swaziland and Mpumalanga—the site is reputed to be some nine hundred million years old and depicts a perfect footprint of the giantess, the Heavenly Princess. "Nomkubhulwane, the Heavenly Princess, is the Zulu goddess of the sky. Once she appeared to me as a young maiden dressed in white. She gave me a prophecy, which I am not allowed to divulge. Nomkubhulwane is the goddess sculpture and offering I created when I had cancer.

"I would like to take you, but I am too frail to climb to the place of the footprint. You must go there, honorable one," he stressed.

Credo gave me directions to the sacred, holy site in the Transvaal, an hour or so away from his compound. Before going on safari I visited this secret, secluded place used for centuries by sangomas and tribal chiefs to do healing work. I came upon the five-foot-long footprint, a natural marvel, a perfect depression in granite; spent the afternoon in spontaneous trance at the healing stone on site; and had visions of the ancient people who worshipped the goddess. Credo had wanted me to see the ancient ones and to take in the energies of this holy, healing, African place.

I reluctantly went on safari as I'd promised Sherry, but as it turned out something amazing happened.

The second week into the tour we were in the Timbavati Game Reserve in the northeastern part of the country bordering Mozambique. Timbavati was famous for its white lions; a rare recessive gene caused their coloring. Worth their weight in gold, breeders and trophy hunters shot and sold them for large sums of money. That morning, from an airplane, shooters using high-powered rifles killed two white males with blue eyes. They were paid $100,000 and $70,000 for the kills.

Our guide, Linda, took us deep into Timbavati to see white lions fenced in by genetic breeders. A big male, more than three hundred pounds, was lying down. His head twitched from side to side. He had a dark tuft on his tail, but his fur was white and his eyes cerulean. I marveled at this unusual and extremely beautiful creature. I'd seen albino animals, but this lion was different. A lioness, not twenty feet away, in a separately fenced off area, was on her back, her hind legs sticking out from her furry belly. She too was white with blue eyes.

That night in the lodge Linda said, "The white lions are viewed in African lore as wisdomkeepers and are considered a gift from the gods to mankind. The Zulus believe their kings transmigrate into lions at death."

Next she showed a video of an African woman named Maria, known as a lion sangoma, or one who could speak to lions and one who understood lions. She was singing to a pride, mesmerizing them, communing with them. As she sang I started singing along in Portuguese—I knew this song! I'd learned it from Pai. Maria sang in her own language. At that moment I was so shocked I thought I might spontaneously start singing it in Zulu. But I kept singing in the language I had learned it. I'd never before imagined anything like this. But my amazement seemed to congeal when I realized, here I am at the border, in Pai's homeland, Mozambique! This song traveled from Africa to Brazil and back here to South Africa through me.

Linda, stunned, asked how I knew the song. I told her about Pai and his ancestors who had arrived in Brazil on slave ships from Mozambique three hundred years before.

When our tour reached Pietersburg, South Africa, I went to an Internet café and e-mailed Ana to tell her about the lion sangoma. "Please ask Pai about the song I learned from him," I wrote. "Tell him I saw the white lions. Does he know about these rare African cats?"

She replied, telling me the song refers to the Orixá Iansã, gold, water, and the earth in Africa. The e-mail concluded with Pai's words: "The white lions are very sacred to us. It is said that when they are all killed, it will be the end of the African people."

A BURIED VEIN OF GOLD

After two weeks I returned to Credo Mutwa's. I saw Ayize walking into the compound with a heavy sack balanced on her head and ran over to her. It slipped, and we both laughed trying to catch it.

"How are you?" I asked.

"I am fine. My shoulder pain is gone."

"What about the big raised thing and the scratches on your back? Are they still there?"

"No. There's nothing. Look how I move my arm." She rolled it at the shoulder and heaved it up toward her ears.

We sat next to a baobob tree with its massive, squat trunk and thick, tapering branches. Ayize seemed vibrant, visibly healthier. She loosened her blouse so that I could see her back. It was completely healed. The raised mound that Virginia and I had seen materialize two weeks ago had vanished. I felt blessed—and humbled—by having been able to help her and grateful for what I'd learned in the healing hut. We hugged then clasped hands in the longest exchange of African handshakes.

At Credo's house he and Virginia were waiting for me at the appointed time. I would spend four days with them before flying on to New York. While I was away on safari the boxes I had sent for from the United States came with clothing for the children. With deftness I'd rarely seen, Virginia plopped down in front of the cases and opened them, strewing the contents all over the floor. She was going to take the clothes to her AIDS clinic and distribute them among her patients. I handed her a personal gift, an ornately appliquéd black lace shawl with silk tassels. She wrapped it around her shoulders, seeming to take to it. Credo unwrapped his present, a book on the Harlem Renaissance, which he wiggled gleefully about.

Virginia brought out a spicy chicken and beef soup. After eating I asked Credo about the white lions.

"For many, many generations, white lions and lionesses, as well as white leopards, were born to lions and leopards in this place, Timbavati, and at one time a white elephant, light, light gray with red tusks was also born there," Credo said. "No one was allowed to come to see these sacred white animals. The people were told the white animals with blue eyes were messengers from God, and if we could be with the animals we would learn the future of humankind by looking into their eyes. But when the white people came, of course, they took the whole country. They made farms there, and some of the farmers, never having seen white lions before, shot these animals and killed them."

Credo didn't budge his massive frame an inch.

"It is said that when a white animal was shot, a tiny shining star fell out of its mouth and floated skyward as the animal died," Credo continued.

He wrapped his shawl tighter against his chest and coughed. He appeared frail. "When the white lion disappears completely, so will all the black people of Africa."

"This is the very same thing Pai said," I told Credo. "Pai knows Timbavati even though he has never been to Africa.

"I was shown a film of Maria the lion sangoma singing to lions," I went on. "I began singing with her; I knew the tune. I knew the song, but the words I sang were in Portuguese."

I sang the melody to Credo and Virginia.

"What about this song Maria sang?" I asked. "Pai taught it to me before I came to Africa, and now I find it's a song from South Africa."

"The song says, ma'am, that Iansã—which means "lady of the waters"—

must come so that we may have peace, that we may have gold." Credo went
on to tell me there was an underground river that ran from Egypt through
South Africa. A buried vein of gold followed the watercourse, and the line
was mirrored in the sky by the stretch of the Milky Way.

"But the song doesn't refer to physical gold," Credo said. "It means
the gold of the spirit. The gold of knowledge. They sing this song in
Mozambique. I met it there, in the land of the Manega and Manebani
people. They sing it also among the Angoni, the Makondeh people
who are famous for their great sculptures in ebony. They sing it among
the Ovengundu people in Angola. I found it in Peru and among these
wonderful, wonderful Native American people, ma'am, who live in
Urubamba."

"Is the melody the same all over the world?" I asked.

"Yes, ma'am," he says. "Funnily enough, it is."

Then Credo told me that he had no successor to follow in his footsteps: "I am like a broken-down truck that goes kerchunk, kerchunk."

I'd read about his life in a book I found in the guesthouse, so I
knew there was a curse on him and his children and his children's children, placed there because he had revealed secret Bantu teachings in his
book *Indaba, My Children*. During the Sharpeville uprising on March
21, 1960, his fiancée was murdered. During the Soweto uprising on
June 16, 1976, he was branded a traitor for revealing the teachings to
white oppressors, and an angry crowd burned his house and stabbed
him nearly to death. He had a history of pain and loss: a son murdered,
his wife dead, his remaining children sick with AIDS. The son who
died had been his chosen successor.

Credo told me he was passing pieces of his knowledge on to certain
people who came to him. Instead of giving it all to one person, he was
sending it out in packets. One of the packets he had passed into my
hands. We made plans for me to return.

On my last day at Naledi, Credo's compound, I went to pay my final
respects. Credo settled himself and looked at Virginia. They nodded.

Time was of the essence as I was about to go to the airport. I had one last thought I wanted to share with Credo.

"With all the wonderful people I've met in Central and South America, I've learned about the gods and ceremonies," I said. "I have seen people healed of terrible diseases. And here with you the knowledge coalesced. Ecstasy is mighty, mighty love. When I touched Ayize tremendous love rushed through me, a bolt of something like light, like the energy from the necklace. I felt this when you said that magical word: Ncumu."

"Wonderful!" he said. "And how do you feel now?"

"I don't have any special capabilities myself, but during ceremony I feel the great force enter me. I want to continue in ceremony. I want to come back and see you again," I said.

"And when you were doing it, did you feel completely at home and fulfilled?"

"Yes, I felt complete. Ecstatic. I know," I told him, unable to say more precisely what I meant but confident he understood, "I most love to be in ceremony. Then I am in the moment where everything is in perfect balance. Ceremony gives me joy and gives my life meaning."

"In life there are exchanges of holy things," Credo said. "He or she who loves is loved in return. He or she who hates is hated in return. What many people don't realize is that a pupil teaches the teacher almost as much as the teacher teaches the pupil."

"That is a very beautiful exchange."

"The work of healing is the holiest work in the whole world," Credo said. "In Africa we are taught that he who heals others is himself healed. If you heal others, you are healed yourself. If you teach others, you are taught yourself."

I thought of the glory of God. Ncumu. Ecstasy.

Then Credo took my hands in his. He said, "Simply be what you are called to be."

EPILOGUE

I had been reluctant to leave Credo and Virginia. A year later I visited them, and, as Credo had promised, the lessons continued. He sent me to different tribes in South Africa and Zimbabwe for teaching. Credo's health is very bad, so I have not seen him recently.

I brought a wildebeest tail from South Africa to give Pai in Brazil. It made the most powerful flywhisk he had ever seen. I have not been initiated into Umbanda; I'm unsure if I ever will be.

It's been nine years, and I am cancer free. I don't have vision in my eye, but I believe in João's work and I've gone back to Brazil and helped Josie with her groups in Abadiânia. When I have time, I sit in the current. Once I brought a picture of Carlos to Brazil. João kissed his photograph. The Brazilians had never seen this happen, ever!

When João de Deus comes to the States, I work alongside Josie and his staff. We see anywhere from 1,400–2,500 people a day. I also take people to the Amazon where I assist Carlos during healings. Both João and Carlos are great healers. I bring patients to them for two reasons: 1) they are sick, or 2) they want to work on their spiritual development. I've learned a lot in South America and Africa and continue learning from João and Carlos. I've also worked with other healers in other countries over the past several years. I have a healing practice in New York. During sessions energy goes into the person I am helping. All the patient needs is contained in the energy, Ncumu. I don't direct it. The body knows what to do with it. As simple as it is, it works.

ACKNOWLEDGMENTS

First and foremost I thankfully remember with gratitude João de Deus and the casa entities; Pai Lazaro and the Orixás; and the High Sanusi Vuzamazulu Credo Mutwa and the Great Ancestors.

This memoir evolved through several drafts, and Jeanne Fleming read them all. Her insightful critiques and unfaltering support meant a lot to me.

Ann Patty is a generous and inspiring editor whose contribution to this book's shape and development has been immense. Thank you.

My grateful admiration to everyone at Inner Traditions, especially editor Meghan MacLean for her integrity and insight.

I thank my family and my daughter for the special support given me. I am appreciative of my friends: Cynthia Beatt, Margaret Bialy, Abiodun Bello, Ruth Boyer, Lara Chkhetiani, Yoko Eishima, Wendy Ewald, Fatima Deen, Jenny Fox, Grace Gunning, Susan Indich, Kevin Jeffries, Sharon Johnston, Jim Kullander, Raimund Kummer, Harlan Matthews, Susan Moran, Andrianna Natsoulas, Lila Pague, Gillian Paolella, George Quasha, Susan Quasha, Gina Rabbin, Elizabeth Randolph, Josie RavenWing, Susan Ray, Carolee Schneemann, Kiki Smith, Shelley Tran, and Rudolph Wurlitzer.

BOOKS OF RELATED INTEREST

Shaking Medicine
The Healing Power of Ecstatic Movement
by Bradford Keeney

The Power of Ecstatic Trance
Practices for Healing, Spiritual Growth, and Accessing the Universal Mind
by Nicholas E. Brink, Ph.D.

Shapeshifting
Techniques for Global and Personal Transformation
by John Perkins

The Shamanic Way of the Bee
Ancient Wisdom and Healing Practices of the Bee Masters
by Simon Buxton

The Voice of Rolling Thunder
A Medicine Man's Wisdom for Walking the Red Road
by Sidian Morning Star Jones and Stanley Krippner, Ph.D.

The Prophet's Way
A Guide to Living in the Now
by Thom Hartmann

The Biology of Transcendence
A Blueprint of the Human Spirit
by Joseph Chilton Pearce

Plant Spirit Shamanism
Traditional Techniques for Healing the Soul
by Ross Heaven and Howard G. Charing
Foreword by Pablo Amaringo

INNER TRADITIONS • BEAR & COMPANY
P.O. Box 388
Rochester, VT 05767
1-800-246-8648
www.InnerTraditions.com

Or contact your local bookseller